THE HEART OF JESÚS VALENTINO

The Heart of Jesús Valentino

A mother's story

EMMA GILKISON

AWA PRESS

First edition published in 2018 by Awa Press,
Level 3, 27 Dixon Street, Wellington 6011, New Zealand.

ISBN 978-1-927249-58-1
Ebook formats
Epub 978-1-927249-59-8
mobi 978-1-927249-60-4

A catalogue record for this book is available from the
National Library of New Zealand.

The author and publisher thank the following for permissions:
The CS Lewis Company Ltd for the quotation on page 187 from
A Grief Observed by CS Lewis © copyright CS Lewis Pte Ltd 1961
Algonquin Books of Chapel Hill for the quotation on page 74 from
The Sound of a Wild Snail Eating by Elizabeth Tova Bailey

The names and personal details of some medical personnel in this book
have been changed at their request.

Cover design by Holly Dunn
Typesetting by Tina Delceg
Editing by Mary Varnham

This book is typeset in Adobe Garamond
Printed by Everbest Printing Investment Limited, China

Produced with the assistance of

Awa Press is an independent, wholly New Zealand-owned company.
Find more of our award-winning and notable books at awapress.com.

EMMA GILKISON graduated in Journalism from Massey University and worked freelance and as a columnist for *The Sunday Star-Times* and *The Dominion*. In 2013 she gained a Bachelor of Applied Arts (Creative Writing) from Whitireia New Zealand. She has studied short fiction and science writing at Victoria University's International Institute of Modern Letters, and her work has appeared in newspapers and magazines. She lives in Brisbane with her partner Roy Costilla and their son Amaru.

*All sorrows can be borne if you put them into a story
or tell a story about them.*

Karen Blixen

For Jesús Valentino
Thank you for helping us bear witness
to all that is beautiful.

Dear Baby

May 2014, Paekākāriki
Dear baby, I am writing to you in front of the ocean. The sun is low but warm on my face and Kāpiti Island is a giant blue cut-out on the horizon. This is what I want to ask you: Would you like me to keep you in my belly until you're born, or would you like me to stop the pregnancy and for us to say farewell now?

Six months earlier I could never have imagined writing this letter. I was trying to conceive. Whenever my period arrived it was like a sad monthly 'Sorry, better luck next time' message. There had been times when I'd thought I was pregnant. My breasts had swelled like water balloons and I was unaccountably tired. I had developed an extraordinary appetite for carrot cake, and hamburgers with beetroot and blue cheese. I was moody and went to pieces after my partner Roy failed to text to tell me he'd be home late for dinner.

There were also times when it seemed so auspicious to conceive I felt sure it would happen. There was the trip Roy and I took over the Peruvian Andes to the Valle Sagrado de los Incas – the Sacred Valley of the Incas – Roy's parents' birthplace. At the pilgrimage site of a local saint we were doused with holy water and our union blessed by a white-robed priest. I mused that if our child were to be conceived in Peru and born in New Zealand, this would be a perfect reflection of his or her dual nationality.

Then there was the unplanned trip after my grandmother's funeral, when our plane was diverted to Christchurch after gale-force winds prevented it landing in Wellington. What seemed at first a major inconvenience turned into an all-expenses-paid romantic overnight stay in a four-star hotel. According to the Fertility Friend Ovulation app on my phone, I was in the middle of my monthly cycle's 'fertile window'.

Whenever my period's due date approached, the wait would be agonising. I'd make frequent trips to the bathroom, hoping for the best. But the stories I'd told myself about our baby's conception remained just that. After a year of trying to conceive, I was feeling worried.

For most of my life until this point my aim had been to avoid pregnancy. One day in the hazy future I might meet Mr Right and we'd have a family, but before then I wanted to find meaningful work, live in France, write a book, start doing yoga every morning, learn to dance salsa, and fulfil a dozen other big and little dreams. Before I knew it, I was thirty-four and single. My mother dropped hints that if I wanted kids I'd better get a move on. Strangers occasionally asked me if I had children: I must have begun to look as though I might be a mother. But no, I'd managed to get the crow's feet around my eyes and the bosom heading south all on my own.

By the time I met Roy, motherhood was well on my radar. Luckily, fatherhood was on his too. We were only a couple of months into our relationship when we stopped using contraception. When I wasn't pregnant after six months I decided to have some tests. By then I was thirty-five, that golden number after which a woman's fertility begins to nosedive, according to a booklet I'd picked up in my doctor's waiting room. A scan and hormone blood test showed up nothing unusual. We were told to keep 'trying' for a year. If we still hadn't conceived we'd be eligible for a publicly funded referral to a fertility clinic.

When the year ended and there was still no baby, I was willing to take the next step. In my younger days I'd thought of fertility treatments as vaguely desperate, the resort of stressed-out executive couples past their baby-making prime trying to force the hand of nature. Now that we were a couple facing infertility things looked rather different.

I decided that after my next period I'd book an appointment with my doctor. It was February, a good time of the year to embark on fertility treatment. Roy and I had spent our summer holiday on the west coast of the South Island, tramping through green forests and drinking in sunsets. We felt rested and in good spirits.

When I realised my period was a few days late, I was lolling about at home, half-heartedly doing research for a newspaper blog. I wondered idly if I should make the ten-minute walk to the pharmacy and pay ten dollars for a pregnancy test and decided I would. It'd probably confirm I wasn't pregnant: I'd been through this rigmarole several times before.

Back home, I collected a urine sample and dipped the stick in the small plastic pot. Almost immediately I thought I saw a positive pink line. Was it a trick of the eye? Too nervous to watch for the several minutes it takes to get a clear result, I left the bathroom. When I came back, there was no mistaking it: the test was positive. I held it before my eyes and walked around the house in circles. Oh my god, oh my god, oh my god. I was truly knocked for six.

I couldn't wait to tell Roy. Should I do this by phone or in person? I decided to wait. It was February 14, Valentine's Day, and we were going out for dinner. I entered my dates into my fertility app to find out when the baby would be due. October 21 happened to be the birthday of my dear friend Amy, the only person I'd told we were trying to conceive. It looked as though I had an auspicious conception story after all.

* * *

Roy threw his arms in the air, swung me around in circles, then kissed me passionately when I told him. This is what I'd like to report. In fact, though, his reaction was one of shock. 'Are you sure?' he said. He had talked about his deep desire to begin a family, but I could see it was taking him a while to process the news.

By now Roy and I had been together for a year and a half. We'd first met two and a half years earlier, on the night New Zealand won the 2011 Rugby World Cup. In the early hours of the morning I'd seen him standing among ecstatic revellers in a packed nightclub, a tall Latino with café-au-lait skin. I was leaving for Mexico on a research project six weeks later, which gave me an excuse to introduce myself. With alcohol-fuelled bravado, I was soon asking him to give me tuition in Spanish.

A couple of weeks later we met at a Mexican restaurant for our first lesson. Over guacamole and corn chips, I learned that he was an economist from Lima, Peru, had lived in New Zealand for five years and worked at the Ministry of Health. A week later I invited him to a Guy Fawkes party at my house. After watching the fireworks, he stayed the night. After three weeks of romance I left for Mexico. I was on cloud nine. Roy had taken up my offer for him to sublet my room in my flat while I was away. He was only recently single. After moving out of his former partner's house he had been staying with a Peruvian friend.

It was too early to say we were in a relationship, but we said we'd look forward to picking things up when I returned. When I arrived in Mexico all I could think of was him. Afraid of appearing needy, I tried to play it cool and emailed him only occasionally. I found myself pursued by a Mexican basketball player, whom I dated, partly to distract myself from thinking about Roy.

When he picked me up at the airport the atmosphere was strained. He'd already moved out of my flat – we'd never planned to live together immediately. A few days later I learned from my flatmate that he'd had a girlfriend staying there. Despite the fling I'd had in Mexico, I was furious and hurt. I felt foolish. I confronted Roy and he fessed up. He was still seeing her. He asked if we could remain friends. I told him it was out of the question.

Six months later, time had mellowed my emotions. When we bumped into each other after work one day, I accepted his invitation to go for a beer and we had an amicable catch-up. I bumped into him at the beach a few days later. Then I bumped into him on the street. Three times in one week – it seemed fate was throwing us back together. And his relationship with the other woman hadn't worked out.

I was cautious, but I couldn't deny I was still attracted to Roy. A few weeks later an Italian movie, followed by pizza, followed by a bottle of red wine at my house, confirmed he felt the same way. He now lived in a villa on the other side of the harbour. He told me he'd stood on the balcony and looked over to my house, singing a love song. This time we took things more slowly but it wasn't long before I felt I was tumbling into love again. I penned a poem: 'His eyes were black angel fish / I swam in their direction and found / his skin was pears baked with cinnamon.'

It wasn't all smooth sailing. A camping trip that summer was a mixture of passionate nights under the stars and arguments in the morning because we had a six-hour drive ahead of us and Roy was swimming rather than helping take down the tent. I discovered he had only a loose relationship with plans and time. I might carefully prepare a meal and he would arrive at nine p.m., having already eaten. My penchant for calm and action lists was shaken up by his unpredictability and disorganisation. We'd grown up in different cultures with different values. On the plus side, he exuded warmth and his positive moods were infectious.

In March, only five months after we'd got together, Roy invited me to Peru to meet his family. He didn't warn me I would be welcomed to the family home with a lunch of roasted guinea pig. His mother, Lucia, had raised the creature herself. It sat on my plate with its claws and snout still attached.

Lucia wore her hair in a short bob, pinned off her broad face with hairclips. Roy had inherited his warm smile from her. His father, Valerio, had bright eyes and thick Elvis Presley hair that he combed to one side. Cancer in his jaw had disfigured the lower part of his face and his speech was a little slurred.

I could see both Lucia and Valerio were immensely proud of Roy, the first in their family to go to university, now living abroad and about to begin a PhD in statistics. They had arrived in Lima as teenage sweethearts, seeking better prospects than there were in Coya, the small village where they'd grown up and where their families eked out an existence growing corn and raising animals. In Lima, Valerio drove taxis and Lucia sold fruit and vegetables in the markets. Through hard work and carefully guarding their money they had bought land and built a house. Later they added extra rooms for rent. They made every sacrifice they could to ensure their sons were well educated. They had named Roy and his brother Ronny after cowboys in an American Western.

I quickly learned Lucia and Valerio had different personal boundaries from the ones I'd been raised with. On a road trip across the Andes to visit their village we had an overnight stop. To save money, they thought all four of us should share a tiny bedroom with two single beds. I offered to cover the bill for two separate rooms. In Coya we stayed with Roy's great-aunt. There was no hot water and her kitchen was a concrete outhouse where she cooked over a fire. Around thirty guinea pigs scampered around the floor devouring food scraps until the day they themselves would become lunch or dinner. Many families in the village lived off the land. It was a humbling experience.

One year after we got together, Roy moved in with me. Although I was in my mid-thirties he was the first partner I'd lived with and there was plenty to adjust to. I had to learn to constructively raise my concerns about his lack of interest in house cleaning, for example. The house became not only messier but also noisier with Roy's loud tuneful whistling and enthusiastic slamming of doors. Yet I knew Roy's presence was changing me in a good way. His smile fast became my welcome-home sign.

We didn't talk a lot about children, but I was thrilled he wanted to start trying. I felt I belonged in this relationship. I wanted a family and I loved the idea of a Peruvian-Kiwi baby.

5 weeks

My GP, Dr Hastie, was very matter-of-fact. 'I might not see you again until you bring your baby in at six weeks for vaccinations,' she said. I'd booked an appointment with her for another pregnancy test and taken Roy with me. Again, the positive pink line had appeared in the small rectangular window of the tester. I could have kissed that pink line. I held the pregnancy test like a winning lotto ticket.

'So you're sure Emma's pregnant?' Roy said, still unconvinced. 'I mean, do the tests ever get it wrong?'

'You've had two positive tests so I think we can be certain Emma is pregnant,' Dr Hastie replied.

Up until this appointment Roy and I had hardly dared believe the pregnancy was real, yet here we were being handed a goody bag stuffed with discount vouchers for baby stores, a sample tub of nappy rash cream, and a flyer promoting a baby sling of all-natural materials. Dr Hastie issued a blood test form, and instructions on how to find a midwife who would be in charge of my care. We exited the practice – Roy and I and our little baby. He or she was currently the size of a sesame seed, according to a pregnancy app I'd downloaded.

Roy immediately wanted to Skype his parents from a dingy alleyway, littered with cigarette butts. I protested this wasn't the right location so he grabbed my hand and marched me up the hill to university, where we found a sofa in a corner of the student hub, near a counter selling cold drinks and snacks. I was quickly swept away by Lucia's and Valerio's reaction to the news. They gasped and beamed from their kitchen in Lima. I realised it wouldn't have mattered if we'd been sitting in a rubbish dump.

'Felicitaciones. Qué buenas noticias,' Lucia said. Her eyes shone like Christmas baubles.

'¡Si son muy buenas noticias, que tocan muy fuerte nuestros corazones! Este es un regalo de Dios. ¡Bendiciones, mucha suerte y buena salud para ustedes!' Valerio said, breaking into one of his soliloquies. What good news that taps strongly at our hearts! This is a gift from God. Blessings, luck and good health to you!

By chance, my mother was flying down from Auckland the next day. She and I were going to spend the weekend in a house by the sea with three of her oldest friends. I picked her up from the airport and we went to meet Roy for lunch at a Malaysian restaurant. As we queued up to order, excitement fizzed inside me. Words began to line up on my tongue… Mum, we've got something to tell you… Mum,

I'm eating for two… Mum, you know how you've been wanting grandchildren?

When she heard the word 'pregnant', Mum gave a sort of a yelp. 'Oh my god. Oh, your baby is going to be so beautiful,' she gasped as she grabbed my arm. Tears glistened in her eyes.

I knew she'd been pining for a grandchild. As a midwife, she had worked with babies for twenty-five years. She had gone on to teach midwifery at university. I knew she would make a fantastic grandmother. Short and sturdy, with a thick bushel of nut-brown hair, my mother is a powerball of energy, whose preferred verb is 'to do'. She is often out cycling at dawn, tends chickens, and writes papers for international conferences. Even when relaxing she plays Sudoku on her phone, looks up the weekend's weather, or books a holiday house for the following summer. She is more level-headed than I am, capable of following an intricate recipe from a *Cuisine* magazine while talking with guests.

'You should get on to finding a good midwife soon. I'll see if I can get any recommendations,' she said excitedly. 'You'll need to decide if you want to have screening tests too.'

'Screening for what?'

'Any abnormalities like Down syndrome or spina bifida. Some people are in favour of screening and others aren't.'

I thought this was a strange thing for her to raise at this early stage, but I supposed she wanted to impart the knowledge of her profession.

'This is such wonderful news, Em. I can't wait to start knitting booties.'

As with the reaction of Roy's parents, my mother's excitement gave me a sense of permission to feel joy too. With each new telling of the news my mind more firmly grasped the reality that I was pregnant. A wanted pregnancy must be one of the loveliest announcements you can make.

* * *

A few blocks back from Ōtaki beach, the holiday house was filled with yellowing books and couches sagging from years of use, well-worn and comfortable. I had known my mother's friends all my life and they had become my close friends as well. Roy and I had decided not to broadcast our news until the pregnancy was further along but I couldn't not tell these women. They celebrated, voiced their approval of Roy, offered me cups of tea while they drank wine, and encouraged me to take another piece of caramel date slice.

Being made a fuss of felt lovely until I went to the bathroom and found small smudges of brown blood on my underwear. I stared. Was this the beginning of a miscarriage? Was my pregnancy going to end when it had barely begun? Or was this just what was called 'spotting'? I'd read that a little bit of blood didn't necessarily mean anything was wrong. But it could. Apparently twenty percent of pregnancies ended in miscarriage.

Trying to appear casual, I mentioned the bleeding to my mother. She said it might be nothing but I could tell she was concerned. Quietly alarmed, I made frequent trips to the bathroom. During the next day there was no blood but in the evening there was more, and this time it was pinker. My stomach churned. I was inwardly miserable. I walked down to the beach, sat on a bench and watched the sun disappear below the horizon. My pregnancy now felt like a lottery.

6 weeks

The next week the small smears and spots of blood kept coming. 'Spotting in early pregnancy' became my most frequent Google search. I discovered the forums where women discuss every intimate aspect of pregnancy. One woman had inexplicably bled throughout her pregnancy and delivered a healthy baby; another had only a little spotting but discovered at the twelve-week scan that her baby was not alive. One night I googled 'brown stringy mucous-like discharge early pregnancy'. Sure enough, I found a woman talking about the same thing.

I learned several things can cause bleeding in early pregnancy. One is 'breakthrough bleeding', when your usual menstrual cycle continues for a while. Another is 'implantation bleeding', which can happen when the fertilised egg implants in the uterus. Many times, doctors don't know the cause. Websites advised me not to worry. The stats are that around twenty percent of women get some bleeding and around fifty percent go on to have normal pregnancies. So I had a fifty-fifty chance. You'd have to be a very 'glass-half-full' person not to be alarmed by those odds.

I decided I needed to see my doctor. Dr Hastie was fully booked so I made an appointment with another in her practice. Roy sat beside me and held my sweaty hand.

Dr Cox nodded as I told her what was happening. 'I've been in a similar situation myself and I know how agonising it is. I can't say if all is well or not. Would you like to have an early scan?'

'Yes, please,' I said.

She requested an urgent appointment. One was available next day. There was a hitch though – while babies' heartbeats can usually be detected at six weeks this is not always the case. We might get a false reading. Alternatively, we could wait and have the scan the following week.

Roy and I discussed the options as we walked back to my office. Throughout the week he had been the sounding board for all my fear. Now he thought we should wait until next week, just to be sure. I decided he was right. I rebooked for the following Wednesday.

That evening I had to work late at the charitable trust where I had a part-time communications job. I was tired and felt overstretched. At eight o'clock I stopped to make dinner. I found I'd been bleeding again, but this time there was more blood and it was redder. This is it, I thought, the start of a miscarriage. Roy was not home yet. I poured myself a large glass of pinot noir and lay down on the couch. And then the bleeding stopped. There was no more that evening. Or the next morning.

My mother called. She had been ringing every second night for updates. 'Can you stop it please?' I said. 'You're stressing me out.'

'Sorry, I just want you to know I'm here for you,' she said.

I registered the hurt in her voice and it irritated me. I knew she cared and just wanted to know if my baby, her first grandchild, was okay. But her hovering was not helping.

A couple of days later I confided in my friend Amy how hard it was sitting on this seesaw of doubt. A few nights earlier I'd had a dream. I was in the bathroom when I passed blood and with it the baby. He was fully formed and wore a white and blue striped jumpsuit. He was small, just a bit bigger than the palm of my hand. He looked at me, gurgling and waving his arms, and I thought he was the most beautiful thing I'd ever seen. Then purple lesions began spreading across his face. His life was faltering before my eyes. My heart was wrenched but I knew there was nothing I could do. He died in my hand.

7 weeks

Running late, Roy and I had filled portable cups with black coffee from our trusty Italian stovetop. The aroma filled the car as we drove to the radiology clinic. When we arrived, a sonographer ushered us into a dimly lit room. As I lay down on the table and she smeared gel across my stomach I breathed deeply, willing myself to accept whatever we were about to find out.

She placed the wand on my belly and almost immediately said, 'There's baby's heartbeat.' A heartbeat! I choked up. I had, I realised, been expecting to hear bad news. Roy and I locked eyes in wonderment. The screen showed a swirl of black and white, like a satellite image of clouds travelling across continents, but in among it was proof that our baby was real.

'Your uterus is retroverted, which means it's tilting backwards, but this should right itself in pregnancy. It looks like it's bicornuate too,' the sonographer said. She explained that usually uteruses are pear-shaped, but bicornuate ones are heart-shaped with two horns, and a wall partially sealing the uterus into two parts. This wall would likely break down as the baby got bigger.

'Bleeding in the first trimester is more common with bicornuate uteruses so that could be what's caused it. You have nothing to worry about from what I can see today. Everything looks like it's progressing normally.'

Roy and I had a skip in our step as we crossed the clinic's parking lot. I started singing the first feel-good tune that came to mind, 'December, 1963' ('Oh, What A Night').

'What a baby, what a scan!' Roy chorused, making me burst into laughter.

Back home, we dropped off the car and headed to work along the waterfront. As I walked Roy grabbed me and perched me side-saddle on his bike. 'Slow down!' I yelled as we careened around bends. He ignored me. As we whizzed through puddles on the road fountains erupted into the air.

8 weeks

There was something noticeably absent in my pregnancy – morning sickness. So far I'd had no reason to rush to the toilet or restrict my diet to bland foods such as bread, potatoes and cheese – the 'beige diet' my friend Rose called it. I vaguely wished I was nauseous so I could feel I truly belonged to the pregnancy club.

I asked Tessa, a midwife, about this when she came to meet us.

'It's nothing to worry about,' she said. 'Your body's probably just adapting well to the influx of pregnancy hormones.'

I felt instantly at ease in Tessa's company. She was a woman of substance. You got the feeling she would be unflappable in an emergency.

'Have a think about whether you'd like me to be your midwife. It's important to get the right fit and it's fine if you want to choose someone else,' she told us. We knew in the first five minutes of meeting Tessa that we wanted her to be our midwife.

'Guess what?' I said to my half-sister Phoebe and her boyfriend Luke. They had come from Auckland to stay with us while Phoebe put on a play she'd written in the Wellington Fringe Festival.

'You're pregnant!' Luke said, with a dramatic flourish.

'Well actually, yes,' I replied.

'Oh, my god!' they said in unison.

Not long afterwards I sent a message to Alex, my half-brother, in Ireland. He and Phoebe are the children of my mother and my stepfather Alistair.

That week we also told the other side of my family: my father Bob, my stepmother Maggie and my half-sisters Eleanor, Meghan and Francie. I am older than these siblings by a long way and have never lived with them, but we resemble each other like a set of Russian dolls.

My father has worked as an early childhood teacher most of his life. He accentuates words for emphasis, narrates with his body and hands, and gives strangers friendly squeezes on the shoulder. He has a long gangly body, and arms that carve great arcs in the air. He wears earrings in one ear and op-shop jackets with badges pinned to the lapel. His hair is usually rumpled and his big brown eyes fill quickly with emotion.

Maggie, a lecturer in early childcare education, is almost the opposite, elegant and self-possessed, with light brown hair cut into a neat bob. She thinks clearly and knows what to say to people at the right time.

Only a month earlier my stepbrother Jacob and his girlfriend Jaimie had announced they were expecting a baby. They were living at Bob and Maggie's house while Jacob got his new African restaurant off the ground.

My parents separated when I was a toddler and I was an only child for the first nine years of my life. But things changed drastically when my mother married Al and when, not long afterwards, my father met Maggie. Over the next seven years I acquired five half-siblings and a stepbrother. All this left me feeling a little displaced. I now had two distinct families but I didn't feel entirely part of either. In my twenties I talked at length to counsellors about this. Occasionally the feeling of not belonging would creep up again. I hoped this baby would bring me closer to both sides of my family.

9 weeks

One night around midnight I began to bleed again. I lay in bed, trying to reconcile myself to the idea that I wouldn't be having this baby after all. By daybreak I'd almost made peace with the situation. I called in to work sick and asked Tessa, now officially our midwife, to organise another scan for that afternoon.

This appointment was at a different radiology clinic. After Roy and I had sat in the waiting room for twenty-five minutes, a short woman with frizzy brown hair appeared. 'Sorry, they just threw people at me and I got behind,' she said tersely.

Almost as soon as the ultrasound wand touched my belly, a heartbeat registered. The sonographer didn't dwell on the baby for long – there were other measurements she wanted to take.

'I can't get a good look because your uterus is retroverted. Bicornuates often cause us problems,' she complained. She found a spot where the bleeding seemed to be coming from. It was just above the egg sac.

'Do you know what might have caused it?' Roy asked.

'I can't tell you,' she snapped.

'So, will the doctor identify the cause?'

'The doctor would be very cross if I said what he was going to do or not do.'

This woman was a caricature of grumpiness but also the bearer of good news. Our baby was the perfect size for its age, she said. The heart rate was bang-on. Everything was all right after all.

After the scan I thought about women in other times and in other places who would not have been able to have these scans and would have had to live with uncertainty. Knowing gives you a sense of control. But was I being overly controlling? I sensed my friend Thomasin thought I was churlish for not having yet broadcast the news of my pregnancy. 'I just told everyone I was pregnant,' she said. 'We didn't even have twelve-week scans and it wasn't built up as such a big deal.'

She was right, I wanted to control who knew and who didn't. Because I didn't have total faith in the pregnancy, my instincts were around self-preservation. I wanted to safeguard myself against potential disappointment, and if that disappointment eventuated I didn't want to share it with the world.

Still the news was good: two positive scans and only three weeks until the twelve-week one. After twelve weeks babies are much less likely to miscarry.

10 weeks

For several months Roy and I had been looking for a house to buy. We had to move out of the one we were renting, which had been sold for the eyewatering sum of three million dollars. This might give the impression we'd been living in luxury, but in fact the 1940s house was run-down. It was its location that made it prime real estate. Perched at the end of a cul-de-sac in the inner-city suburb of Mt Victoria, it had sweeping views of the harbour.

The new owner planned to demolish the house and build his family's dream home. The demolition date wasn't set but was likely to be in the next few months. Our rental was going to be a hard act to follow we discovered as we traipsed around open homes. Online descriptions and carefully angled photos rarely matched the reality. Plus, our budget placed us at the lower end of the Wellington property market and competition was fierce. In four months we'd already made three unsuccessful offers.

Our hopes were now pinned on a house in the hillside suburb of Melrose. It was a solid weatherboard dwelling, built by the elderly man who still lived in it. He had raised his family there but was now on his own. The interiors were like a 1960s' time warp, a retro look that had recently become fashionable again. From the lounge there was a view of the southern part of the city, with Cook Strait a crumpled scarf of blue in the distance.

The deadline for tenders was fast approaching. We tallied the numbers again and again to work out how much we could offer. We had to take into account not only what the bank would lend us, but what we could afford in mortgage interest payments once our baby arrived and I was no longer in paid work. Money would be tight.

When we arrived to present our offer, we told the real estate agent the owner would be welcome to come back and visit his old house any time he wanted. Later that day we heard we were $50,000 short of the winning offer.

A few days later we made an offer on a house we'd seen only the day before tenders closed. In the suburb of Brooklyn, it was a grand old villa with a flat underneath that had fallen into disrepair. It was within our price range because of the extra income we'd get from renting the flat. I thought about the skylights we could put in the ceiling to let in more light and imagined strolling down the Brooklyn hill into town.

We missed out again, this time by $500. It was excruciating to come so close and still lose. Every time we made an offer on a house, we imagined ourselves living there. It seemed a necessary part of the process, but becoming emotionally invested made losing out all the harder.

11 weeks

I sat in the car and drummed my fingers on the steering wheel. Our appointment was at nine a.m. and it was now eight-forty-seven. I'd had to chivvy Roy out of bed. As usual he'd allowed himself the minimum amount of time to get ready. While I waited he was fixing himself a takeaway Peruvian breakfast – canned tuna mixed with diced red chilli, sliced onion and lemon juice on toast.

'Roy, I'm sick of you always making us late,' I said as he got in the car.

'Please don't start with this attitude, Emma, not today. This is a really important appointment for us.'

As we left our street Roy realised his breakfast was still sitting in a container on the kitchen bench. I bit my tongue and sighed. The fact I was irritated with Roy rather than fixated on the coming scan showed I was feeling quite relaxed about it. Although called the twelve-week scan, you can have this procedure from eleven weeks. I was now eleven weeks and three days pregnant. The scan represented a kind of finish line. It looked like we'd finally made it.

My heart sank when the grumpy sonographer from our last scan called out my name. To avoid her I had booked at a different clinic, but it turned out sonographers rotated between clinics.

'Damn,' I mouthed to Roy as we followed her down the passageway.

With my stomach lathered in gel, the sonographer quickly found the baby and a heartbeat. She began taking the screenshots and measurements.

'Your bladder is empty, which makes things difficult. You were supposed to drink water before you came,' she tut-tutted.

'Should she drink a glass of water now?' Roy said.

'No. Then I'd have to wait for an hour and a half for it to get to her bladder,' she scolded.

She turned to me. 'Your uterus is still retroverted, which makes it harder. You should have waited and had the scan at thirteen weeks.'

She decided she'd have to do an internal examination, in which the probe is inserted vaginally. More images came up on screen: baby's brain like a little walnut; a spine like train tracks; a stamp of a bottom. Body parts were much more distinguishable now. Our baby was wriggling around a lot and this was annoying the sonographer but I found it wonderful. There was my clever little one, turning over, moving an arm, swimming about its little pool.

'It doesn't like to stay still, just like its father,' I said.

It looked as though the baby was practising boxing, with a little fist punching just above its chest. Was that what it was? No, it couldn't be, I decided. An arm was clearly visible at its side. The sonographer was looking at the same thing – a pulsating blob, mid-sternum.

'I've never seen anything like that before,' she said. Her voice had gone quiet. 'All I can tell you is that this is very unusual. I can't tell how much of a cause for concern it is.'

She went to see if a doctor was available, but none were. We would, she said, need to see the hospital's maternal foetal medicine team for an assessment.

At the reception desk a staff member gave us a folder containing a picture of our baby and a disc of images. These are souvenirs given to all parents at the twelve-week scan. In the picture our baby was lying on his back. Clearly visible on his chest was a small round orb.

As we left the clinic, I felt more taken aback than worried. Roy was the same. 'We don't know what this means. We'll just have to wait for the specialist appointment,' he said.

When I got home my mind kept returning to the scan. Could that orb above our baby's chest possibly be his heart? I Googled my suspicions: '12-week scan baby with heart outside of chest'. I immediately got an answer from Wikipedia:

Ectopia cordis is a congenital malformation in which the heart is abnormally located either partially or totally outside of the thorax. In most cases, the heart protrudes outside the chest through a split sternum… The occurrence of ectopic cordis is 8 per million births…. In general, the prognosis for ectopia cordis is poor – most cases result in death shortly after birth due to infection, hypoxemia, or cardiac failure.

I scrolled through other websites and saw images I couldn't help but recoil from. They included a dead baby with an uncovered heart on its chest. I knew I shouldn't be leaping to a diagnosis but the possibility hit me. I wept.

A montage of images began playing in my mind. Me fronting a YouTube clip to raise money for an expensive life-saving operation, saying, 'We're just an ordinary couple and we never thought this would happen to us, but we love our baby and want to give him or her the best chance of survival.' A huddle of doctors in white coats animatedly discussing our baby's condition. A funeral at Old St Paul's with a tiny coffin, and Roy and I in the front row, leaning against each other in our grief.

Although I knew I shouldn't jump to conclusions, questions began to form in my mind. Would I be offered a termination if this was a potentially fatal condition? What were the chances a baby with ectopia cordis would survive surgery?

Later that afternoon Tessa called with information relayed to her by the doctor who had looked at the scans. She confirmed it was the baby's heart we had seen outside the chest. My conclusion had been right. A referral had been made to the maternal foetal medicine specialist team and we'd be contacted early next week with an appointment. Our baby was one of the eight in a million.

I called Roy and picked him up from the university. When he got into the car he hugged me tightly and began to cry. 'This is bad news, Emsy,' he said. We decided to go for a walk. Night had fallen. The city was shrouded in fog, and street lamps cast a blurry yellow light. We drove to a city lookout but could see only a few metres in front of us.

'Did Tessa say what causes this condition?' Roy said.

'No, it sounds like nobody exactly knows. If the baby has even a slim chance of living I think we have to take it.'

'It's too early to say things like that. We need to wait to hear what the specialist says.'

I knew Roy was right. I promised to try and suspend judgement. 'I'm so glad we have each other,' I said. And I was. The warmth of Roy's embrace and the knowledge that whatever happened we'd still have our love for each other was the only thing that gave me some hope.

I proposed going out for dinner. We found a table at a cosy Burmese restaurant decorated with golden Buddhas and ornate wooden carvings. We ordered exotic dishes: a herb pancake filled with prawns and chicken, tangy with lemongrass; a fish curry cooked in banana leaves. I wanted distraction, transportation to foreign places.

'We are not meant to touch hearts. Hearts are away, hidden, at the centre where they can't be got at. Protected. Vital. … When a surgeon opens a ribcage and mends a heart, it is a miracle. Otherwise we do not touch,' Louisa Young writes in *The Book of the Heart*.

An ectopia cordis heart is quite the opposite to this. It is a heart revealed, open to the elements, able to be touched. Before I became used to the idea, it was disturbing to imagine my baby's heart beating outside his body. Perhaps for some the idea is grotesque. A Babylonian tablet from 2000 B.C. bears the inscription: 'When a woman gives birth to an infant that has the heart open and has no skin, the country will suffer calamities.' Could this refer to a baby with ectopia cordis?

In medical terms, I learnt, ectopia cordis results from a failure of proper maturation of midline mesoderm and ventral body wall formation during embryonic development. It took me some time to decipher what this meant. At around six weeks' gestation, the embryo is eight millimetres long and shaped like the sole of a shoe. After its spine has formed, the two sides of the embryo (the ventral walls) fold inwards towards each other. The sides meet and fuse down the front centre (midline) of the embryo, like the closing of a purse. When this fusion takes place, the mesoderm layer forms muscles, tissues and bones. If the mesoderm layer doesn't meet perfectly in the middle, abnormalities occur, a common one being cleft palate.

With ectopia cordis, the mesoderm layer of the throat, chest or abdomen doesn't fuse properly, and the heart is left outside. It's not known why this happens. A gene, yet to be identified, could be involved. So could environmental factors. One theory holds that the heart has not formed in the correct position to begin with and therefore the mesoderm layer cannot seal around it.

After birth the prognosis is poor: the assaults of the world are too much for an uncovered heart. In many cases the heart has other defects. Most babies die shortly after birth due to infection, cardiac failure or lack of oxygen. Texas Children's Hospital estimates that ninety percent of ectopia cordis babies are stillborn or die within the first three days of life. Due to the rarity of the condition and the short lifespan of the babies, few treatment options have been developed. Yet there are success stories. Surgery has been carried out to create a nest in the chest where the baby's heart can sit and skin grafts used to seal over it.

I found a clip on YouTube of a toddler called Audrina, who was born in January 2013 with ectopia cordis and was saved by a team of American doctors. She wore a pink plastic corset to shield her heart for several months after surgery and was reported to be doing well. Closer to home in New Zealand, Aisha Te Kani was born in 1980 with ectopia cordis and operated on. Aisha is now thirty-five. Her pulsating heart is clearly visible beneath its skin graft but otherwise she leads a normal life. In a newspaper story, Aisha is quoted saying a woman in a clothes shop once thought her heart was a ferret and was waiting for it to jump out from her top.

12 weeks

Before I could get the words out I'd started to cry. I'd gone to see Thomasin, not only a friend but in some ways a surrogate mother, craving her warm enveloping presence. I carried the blue folder containing the picture of our baby from the twelve-week scan. Telling her about his heart had reconnected me with the gravity of the situation, the shock, the unfathomability. When I calmed down we drank lemon verbena tea and talked through the next steps.

Thomasin now thought we'd been right not telling many people I was pregnant. Still there were maybe a dozen people who did know. Sometimes, when I told them about the baby's heart, I found myself resisting being pulled into the maelstrom of 'This is a calamity'. Nothing was a foregone conclusion yet, I told myself.

The appointment with the maternal foetal medicine specialist team had been booked for Thursday, the day before the Easter holiday. I was hoping the doctors would tell us more about possible surgery. Thursday was also the day the tender closed for another house in Melrose that we were considering making an offer on. The house was a two-storeyed weatherboard 'home and income' that overlooked the zoo. It was run-down but had potential. The question was how much would we have to invest and what was practical? Could we knock down walls to open up the dingy kitchen? Could the second lounge be turned into a bedroom? We were interested but cautious. We decided to pay four hundred dollars to commission a builder's report. The timing was tight. The builder would assess the property on Tuesday and we would receive his report on Wednesday. This would give us a day to think about our offer.

On Wednesday night a ferocious storm hit the city. Rain pummelled down outside as Roy and I sat mulling over the builder's report. It didn't look good. The house's foundations were cracked and would require about twenty-five thousand dollars to fix. A structural engineer would need to be brought in, the whole house jacked up and the foundations re-poured. There were issues with an old chimney, and dampness was creeping into the ground floor apartment from the bank behind it.

With a baby coming a demolition site might be the last thing we needed. On the other hand, if we lost the baby we might need a project to throw ourselves into. Deciding whether to put an offer on the house felt like peering into a crystal ball. We said we'd sleep on it. I switched on the telly and Roy began working on his PhD.

An hour later we heard thunder. But was it thunder, or a truck emptying a load of gravel nearby? Then we heard a sickening crunch. This sound was close. I pulled back the curtain and peered out into the garden. It was difficult to see through the inky darkness and lashing rain but it looked as though our white picket fence had disappeared. We rushed outside. Yes, the fence and a few metres of our garden were gone. At the edge of the property, where formerly there had been a steep bank, a large amount of earth had cascaded down on to the property below.

'I'll call Juan. He'll know what we should do,' Roy said. His friend Juan worked as an architect for the council.

Juan advised Roy to call 111. Ten minutes later half a dozen firemen in yellow suits appeared. We went back outside to survey the damage. The cause of the slip was now evident: water was gushing from a large broken pipe in the bank.

'Council engineers are on their way to assess the damage. The house below is being flooded,' one of the firemen said. 'You may as well wait inside.'

Half an hour later there was a knock at the door. It was now ten p.m. A burly man in a fluoro vest introduced himself as Joe. 'Look, we may have to evacuate you,' he said. 'We're worried there could be another slip that would undermine your house's foundations.'

I phoned and woke my father, who said we could stay at his house if we needed to. Just after eleven Joe knocked on our door again. 'Sorry, but you're going to need to pack your bags and leave straight away.'

Everyone at Dad's was asleep. Their dog, a tiny French butterfly-Affenpincher cross named Oska, began barking wildly and racing around us in tight circles. Dad got up and made us a cup of tea. It was midnight by the time, tired and stunned by the evening's events, we got into the two squeaky single beds in my sisters' old room and turned off the light.

Next morning at seven-thirty I got a text from Tom Hunt, a reporter at *The Dominion Post*. He'd received reports from Civil Defence about the damage being wreaked by the storm and realised my house was the one evacuated. As a former journalist, I knew he wanted the 'victim's experience'. I called him and quickly explained what'd happened. Shortly afterwards Joe rang to say a government agency, EQC, needed to inspect our property. There had been no more slips in the night, but they wanted to make sure the earth beneath the house was stable. 'Hard to say when the engineers will be available,' he said. 'You probably won't be back home until after Easter.'

This would mean five nights away from home. As I digested the news, I worried about our specialist appointment that afternoon. I had no idea what kind of state we'd be in afterwards. We could stay at Dad's, but I'd rather have our own space where we could unfold emotionally.

'Joe,' I said, 'it's a really bad time for us to be away from home. Is there anywhere we could stay?'

'I can't promise anything,' he said, 'but the council may be able to put you up somewhere. I'll look into it.'

Meanwhile, TV1 and TV3 were trying to get in touch via Twitter and Facebook. I wasn't interested in being a poster child for the storm: I needed to be mentally ready for our hospital appointment. I tried to underplay the drama of the slip. Yes, it was a nuisance, but we weren't hurt.

By mid-morning Joe had organised a motor lodge for us to stay at. I was allowed back into our house to pack some things. When I arrived, there was a cluster of men wearing orange hard hats traipsing through our garden. I went inside and got to work. Phone chargers, work notes, toiletries, walking shoes: as I placed the items in my suitcase there was a knock at the door.

It was Joe. 'Sorry to muck you around but EQC have done their assessment already. You've got the all-clear to come back home.'

'There's no danger of another slip?'

'Doesn't look to be. Sorry about the change of mind.'

'Don't worry,' I said. 'This is good news.'

I drove back across town and collected Roy from Dad's. Aside from part of our section being cordoned off with red tape stating 'DANGER ZONE – DO NOT ENTER', life could go back to normal.

Our hospital appointment was at three, but when we went to leave our car was blocked by three large trucks belonging to the council contractors who were securing the bank below our property. Moving the trucks took five minutes. Another truck was blocking the turning bay at the bottom of the street. Rain was still pouring down, obscuring my view through the rear window. Roy got out of the car and shouted instructions, which only made me more anxious. I knew we were now running late and I was in tears. Finally, one of the contractors, a stocky Māori with dreadlocks and a big smile, offered to help. Right in the middle of the road he stripped off his muddy gumboots and wet weather gear, jumped into the car and manoeuvred it out of the road.

Although we were fifteen minutes late for our appointment the receptionist didn't seem concerned. Tessa, too, was waiting patiently. We were ushered into a dimly lit ultrasound room for another scan before meeting the specialist obstetrician. This time the sonographer was in her mid-twenties. Her dark hair was scraped back into a tight bun and her eyebrows were carefully plucked into two thin commas. She issued short curt questions and statements. Did we want to see the screen? Did we want her to tell us what she was seeing?

The baby was sleeping. No one said much as we watched his body parts and his heart, pulsing above his chest, come into focus. The sonographer scanned around the abdomen. I suspected this was to check if any other organs were spilling out, which I'd read sometimes happened when the whole of a baby's midline was open. The stomach looked normal.

'Dr D will see you in a few minutes after she's looked at the pictures,' the sonographer said as she finished up.

Dr D introduced herself and Louise, the clinic midwife. The doctor was only a bit older than me and had pixie looks: olive skin, brown eyes and hair that was cropped short. Her neck was encircled by a fine gold chain. Louise was older, with black hair cut into a decisive bob, and chic trousers. They made a glamorous pair, more glamorous than you'd expect to find in a hospital. There was a third member of their party, a student registrar. That meant there were six of us seated at a round table in a small, slightly stuffy meeting room.

'I can confirm your baby has ectopia cordis. His heart is outside his sternum,' Dr D said.

'He?'

'Yes, I'm fairly certain your baby is a boy.'

Dr D said she had seen two other babies with this condition. One was terminated and one was carried to full term 'for religious reasons'.

'That baby had other organs outside his body and died soon after birth. Ectopia cordis is a condition incompatible with life. If you continue the pregnancy your baby will not survive.' She spoke in a clear, neutral way, a voice for relaying difficult information.

'But what about the option of surgery?' I asked.

'There is no known procedure to operate,' she said.

I told her about the cases of ectopia cordis we'd seen on the internet where babies had survived. 'Wouldn't you try to do something if there was even a little bit of hope?' My voice cracked and tears rolled down my cheeks.

'Well, if surgery was attempted it would have to be at Auckland's Starship Hospital. I can ask them if they'd be willing to see you.' She sounded unpersuaded. 'There is also a high rate of stillbirth with these babies.'

'What is the rate?'

'I can't say exactly. The condition is too rare for good statistics to have been recorded.'

'Can you direct us to more information?'

'There are mostly only case studies available. There aren't international stats as such. You also have the option to terminate.'

'No doubt you'll need to think about it,' Louise interjected. 'We can meet again.'

We left the clinic and stood at the top of the elevator with Tessa. 'I wish they'd had more information about the condition,' I said. 'I don't think Dr D would have mentioned surgery if I hadn't asked.'

'Maybe because it's such a longshot,' Roy said.

'But what about the girl whose heart was put back in her chest in Texas? We've got to do the best we can for our baby,' I said.

Faced with the doctor's lack of optimism, I suddenly understood why mothers say they would walk to the ends of the earth to protect their children.

'I think you have to do what's best for you, as well as the baby,' Tessa said. 'You need to think of your own needs too and what you're able to deal with.'

I could see she was right. We wouldn't be serving the baby by choosing a course of action we weren't strong enough to cope with. That was the counterbalance to the idea that we should do anything we could for the sake of the baby, no matter how hard.

The hospital chapel was a small room with a wall of bright stained-glass panels. Roy had suggested we visit it. I went straight to a small tapestry of Jesus, looking for the image of the sacred heart, but Jesus was nailed to the cross and his heart was bleeding.

We fell into chairs in front of a silhouette of the cross. We were suddenly hit with the force of the choice we'd been given. We could terminate the pregnancy, or continue it knowing the baby was likely to die. I felt overwhelmed by the two awful options.

'We need to ask God or nature to make this choice for us,' I said. 'Or the baby needs to decide. I love him and I don't think I can make this decision.'

'Our son,' Roy began. He laid his head in my lap and cried. It was one of those moments when time ceases to exist. I heard the rustle of someone entering the chapel but didn't look up. About five minutes later a chaplain approached us. I guessed she was in her thirties. She wore a long-sleeved purple T-shirt, and a mother-of-pearl cross around her neck.

'I couldn't help noticing you are in distress,' she said quietly. 'Would you like me to sit with you?' I think Roy may have been about to say no, but I found myself telling her about our baby.

She listened, her forehead creased in empathy. 'What a very difficult position you are in. I can't imagine how hard it is. Would you like me to pray with you?'

We nodded.

'Heavenly Father, we pray for your presence. We pray for your love and support of Emma, Roy and their baby in this very, very difficult time. We pray for strength for them. And we pray for your guidance, so they will know exactly what to do. May they also know how very loved they are by you.'

Giving us her card, she told us we could call if we wished to see her again.

That night, exhausted, I went to bed before Roy. Alone in the dark, my mind filled with images of the two harrowing possibilities our baby faced. I let out deep, gut-wrenching sobs. After a while I went and found Roy in the lounge. He'd fallen asleep in front of television. He came to bed and held me tight in his arms. That night we made love twice. Perhaps we were trying to use physical connection to assuage the pain.

Good Friday dawned clear and calm. I rang Clarinda, an old and dear friend in Nelson, to tell her about my pregnancy and the baby's heart. Her response seemed guarded. I understood why when she shared her own news. 'Em, I'm pregnant too.'

Unlike my baby, Clarinda's was not wished for. Clarinda was torn by trying to decide whether to terminate. Her voice dipped and rose with doubt and anguish. She had broken up with the baby's father and he was now sending her texts saying, 'This is the biggest mistake you'll ever make' and 'You are killing our baby.'

'But Em,' she said, 'I don't love him and I don't want to have a baby on my own. I'd have to abandon my Masters degree. The timing is so bad.'

She had sought out a tarot card reader for advice. The reader said that, if she aborted, her baby's soul would be okay. The soul was a robust thing. The reader herself had had an unwanted pregnancy and had meditated and communicated with the baby in utero, seeking its approval to abort. The baby had said, 'Okay, my soul will wait for you.' The next time she'd got pregnant she had again had doubts, but this time the baby's soul was insistent it wanted to be born so she'd kept the baby. If Clarinda decided to abort, she said, her baby's soul might later return to her too.

Does a baby have a soul in the womb? Do souls endure, and do they have powers to determine when and how they born? These were exactly the kind of questions I wanted answers to. Would my baby be born again with a mended heart if I aborted now?

Mine and Clarinda's situations were parallel in that we both had to decide whether to terminate, yet at the same time they were weirdly inverse. Clarinda wasn't trying for a baby, didn't want a baby and wasn't in love with the baby's father. I had tried for a baby for a year, wanted a baby and was in love with the baby's father. Yet my baby was likely to die.

Roy wanted to Skype his parents. I knew we needed to do this but I dreaded telling the story again. I needn't have worried. Lucia and Valerio were as always big-hearted and empathetic. Valerio told me to calm myself, to look for peace rather than be swept up in the drama and sadness of the situation.

Roy spent the rest of the morning watching re-runs of old-school Christian movies on the net. He told me this reminded him of his childhood, when watching religious movies at Easter was de rigueur. Like most Peruvians, Roy was raised Catholic. I could tell he was finding comfort in returning to his roots.

'Emsy, I think we should go to Easter Sunday mass tomorrow,' he said.

'Okay,' I said.

I wasn't raised in any religion. A spiritual dilettante, I've collected ideas, images and rituals from many different traditions. I have a statuette of the Virgin Mary on the mantelpiece. Occasionally I pray to God, Archangel Michael and any other celestial beings who may be listening. Sometimes I kneel on the floor of my bedroom and do a form of Buddhist chanting originating from Japan. I have a collection of tiny ceramic skeletons I bought in Mexico on the Day of the Dead, one of the most breathtaking celebrations I've ever witnessed, when the spirits of our ancestors are said to pass through the veils and visit us. I believe there is truth and beauty in the essence of all the world's major religions. The basic tenets of how to be a kind, peace-loving human being are good ones. I believe in a divine force of consciousness called God but I am not attached to the stories or rites of any particular religion. I believe the stories are metaphors created by different cultures in different times, to help people understand the same universal phenomena. Maybe there'd be a message for us in Easter's themes of suffering, death, rebirth and resurrection. Easter Sunday also happened to be my birthday.

* * *

Next morning Roy woke me with a birthday serenade and a breakfast of croissants and jam, fresh pineapple and mango. We'd arranged to go to mass with my father and stepmother. When I arrived at the cathedral I was happy to learn it was called Sacred Heart. I'd already begun imagining my baby's heart like the images you see of Jesus and Mary with their hearts on the outside, encircled with light.

The cathedral was handsome, with grand arches and Grecian pillars. The walls and ceiling were painted the light shades of pink you see at dawn. Behind the pulpit hung a painting of Jesus in white robes, his hands gesturing towards his heart while angels waved incense around his feet. Above the painting, near the church eaves, was a giant heart sculpted from white stone.

As the mass began the priest announced there were to be six babies baptised. They came forward, carried in their parents' arms in snow-white gowns that cascaded about their tiny bodies. I wasn't prepared for this. If Dr D was correct, my baby wouldn't have a future like these babies. As the priest spoke and the choir sung hallelujah, my eyes blurred with tears.

Two young boys were sitting with their father in the pew in front of us. The elder one, who was about six, gazed at me quizzically. No doubt he was wondering why the grownup was crying. At the part of the service when everyone said, 'Peace be with you' and shook hands with their neighbours, the younger boy reached out his hand to Roy. The gesture felt so poignant. I sobbed into Roy's shoulder as the service ended.

'Shall we go and talk to the Father?' Roy said. 'Maybe we can get an appointment to see him.' As people milled about in the foyer with cups of tea, we introduced ourselves to the priest and asked if we could make a time to meet.

'Ah, you're getting married?' he asked.

'No, we… It's about a baby,' I stammered. Quickly I explained. The father took my hand in his warm well-padded one. He suggested we meet next morning.

In the afternoon Roy took me to pick up my birthday surprise. It was a retro ladies bike, ruby red with a basket on its front handlebars. I picked out a mauve helmet. That night my father cooked me a birthday dinner. It was a warm gathering that included Clarinda, who'd come to Wellington unexpectedly for a family funeral. She gave me a piece of rose quartz carved into a tiny angel. The quartz was opalescent pink, the crystal of the heart. I instantly claimed it as a talisman.

The next day we met Father Lyons in the cathedral. He removed his tweed cap, revealing the shiny patina of his balding head. 'Thank you for asking to meet with me,' he said, leading us to a small chapel off the side of the main church.

I prepared to explain our baby's condition, but not only had the priest recalled our conversation, he'd done some research on ectopia cordis and contacted one of his parishioners, a paediatric surgeon. He understood our baby was likely to die. Roy told him the option we'd been given of ending the pregnancy.

'Our thinking has moved on from the old days when we said a terminated baby's soul would go to purgatory. An aborted baby would go back to God,' Father Lyons said in a gentle voice. 'But I think your baby would prefer to live, however briefly.'

'Father, how could we inflict that suffering on our child? He'd have to face death as soon as he was born,' Roy said.

The priest looked at us carefully. 'Then again he may not experience this as a suffering at all. He would be received directly into the arms of God and the angels.'

What about our suffering, I thought. If we chose to continue the pregnancy, wouldn't we be opening up to an enormous grief that might rip us apart?

As if he'd read my thoughts, Father Lyons said, 'God never presents us with challenges that are too hard to handle. You would not be left to suffer alone. I know this may sound far-fetched, but it is kind of a privilege to have a baby with such a rare heart. You may even find there are unexpected blessings in this experience.'

He asked our permission to pray for an intercession in the name of Mother Mary Aubert, the nun who had founded Wellington's Home of Compassion. Mother Aubert had a love of children, taking in orphans and babies left on her doorstep. The Catholic Church of New Zealand was petitioning Rome to have her canonised and she was likely to become New Zealand's first saint.

Standing before the pulpit in the main part of the church, Father Lyons then anointed us with a rose-smelling oil applied to our foreheads and palms. 'I'll pray for a miracle. I can't guarantee what form that miracle will take and whether it will mean the survival of your baby.'

Afterwards he gifted us a book of prayers he had compiled called *You Visited Me* and a card depicting Mary with her son Jesus.

'Can I borrow a bible, Father?' Roy said.

I was embarrassed by his request, but the priest considered it for only an instant before saying yes. He led us through a passage into the innards of the church where candlesticks were stacked with boxes of wafers and found a spare bible. As we said our goodbyes he said, 'This is a great challenge and the way you respond to it will affect the rest of your lives.'

Afterwards we sat in the sunshine on the steps in front of the church. Even though I wasn't Catholic, the meeting had left me filled with calm, peace and a new kind of hope. Maybe this was a challenge we could face.

13 weeks

'Did you get the birthday card I sent?' Mum asked over a cup of tea and a feijoa cake she'd baked. 'The funniest thing happened when I posted it.'

Before our baby's diagnosis I'd booked a week's leave from work after Easter. The plan was to spend it with my family in Auckland and the Coromandel. The timing had worked out perfectly. It was a relief to be in my mother's care.

She explained she'd planned to include with the card our spare house key, which she'd taken accidentally the last time she stayed with us. Rummaging through the contents of her handbag looking for the loop of red ribbon attached to the key, something else red had caught her eye. When she fished it out, it turned out to be a heart-shaped red felt brooch, embroidered with tiny beads. It had belonged to my grandmother who had died the year before. She'd felt a tingle discovering the brooch and had decided to give it to me, pinning it to the birthday card. I hoped the card would arrive safely.

'I hope you don't mind but I've started knitting something,' she said. She produced a half-finished baby's sleeping bag, purple with flecks of yellow and blue. I was temporarily undone by the thought our baby might never get to snuggle in the sleeping bag.

'I'm sorry,' she said. 'I shouldn't have…'

'No, Mum, it's okay. It's lovely.'

I could tell she was full of her own grief about her grandchild. She tried to conceal it but every now and then I would see a wan look in her eyes.

Later in the afternoon I showed her and my sister Phoebe the video footage of the twelve-week scan, with the baby's heart bouncing like a tiny ball outside of his chest. They gazed sadly at the screen, not saying much. I found myself cutting through the maudlin silence. 'I want to be as positive as I can for my baby's sake,' I said defiantly.

It was a black night and the road to Coromandel was windy as we drove to a beach house where we were to spend a few nights. The house belonged to a patient of Al, who was a GP. Trust between Al and me had not always come easily and usually I didn't open up to him, but as we drove I quizzed him on what happened when New Zealanders needed operations overseas.

'Could we go to the States for surgery for our baby's heart if it wasn't available here?'

'There is a limited pool of public health funding for overseas treatment. They choose who gets the surgery based on likelihood of success and the impact on quality of life. Surgery on ectopia cordis would be risky,' he said.

'So not likely to rate well?'

'No, probably not.'

'What would it cost if we were to pay for the operation ourselves?'

'Phew, maybe $100,000. A lot.'

'But wouldn't there be specialists around the world who would want to research his heart, seeing the condition's so rare?'

'Unfortunately, rare conditions don't tend to be well researched. You need a big pool of people to research and the potential to positively influence a great many lives.'

I imagined trying to raise $100,000 for a heart operation. Babies in less privileged countries died every day of diseases that could be cured for a fraction of that.

Ōpito Bay faces north-east, a neat crescent of white sand. I couldn't sleep the night we arrived. At one-thirty in the morning I wandered out on to the deck and stared up at the night sky. In that moment I felt that in the grand scheme of things whatever happened with our baby everything would be okay. In the immensity of the universe this event could be absorbed.

I had the same feeling after we climbed a bluff the next day to a Māori pa site. The sea, dotted with dark green islands, sparkled all the way out to the horizon. That day I'd discussed with Mum the plight of communities affected by a cyclone in the Solomon Islands. Chile had just had a massive earthquake. Compared to such tragedies and loss, maybe losing a baby would be bearable. In Tibetan Buddhism there is a concept called sems pa chen po – the vast and spacious mind. The belief is that if you cultivate this kind of mind and see your personal pain within the bigger picture, you will reduce your own suffering.

It was early evening by the time we returned and I swam in a sea turned pink from the reflections of the sunset. It was incredible that it was warm enough to be swimming in May, the last month of autumn.

I swam again the next morning. Afterwards, I sat on the beach and thought about the baby. Had we been given him for a reason? Did we have something to learn from him? Did he already have a soul? Do souls choose their parents? Had the baby chosen to pass through this world fleetingly, as an entry point to somewhere else he needed to go? If so, was it my responsibility to let his destiny unfold by bringing him to full term?

I sat weeping quietly for a while, sifting the warm golden sand through my fingers. I asked myself how the decision to end the pregnancy felt inside. Empty and regretful. And continuing? This possibility gave me energy and hope. Tentatively, I decided I wanted to keep the baby. Up until then Roy and I had talked in hypothetical, almost neutral terms about whether to terminate or continue the pregnancy. When I arrived back in Wellington I would lay my cards on the table.

14 weeks

Roy had cooked a welcome-home dinner of Peruvian stir-fried beef with chilli, tomatoes, onions and rice. As we ate he gave me some news. 'Alix has been working in a children's hospital in Philadelphia in the cardiac unit. She's seen babies like ours where they've attempted surgery.'

Alix was a former girlfriend of Roy's who was now working as a doctor in the States. It was amazing to know someone with first-hand knowledge of ectopia cordis, but Alix's feedback was not optimistic. She had emphasised to Roy there was only a slim chance of our baby surviving surgery, and talked about the intensive and ongoing medical care required if he did.

'After heart surgery babies have to be fed intravenously for months, and because of that there is a higher risk of infection, so they pump them full of antibiotics,' Roy reported. 'They may not be able to breathe unassisted. It all puts a lot of stress on couples. Alix has seen some people crack under it.' I had a flash of Roy and I arguing in a hospital corridor under bright fluorescent lighting as orderlies hurried past.

Alix had contacted another doctor friend, a geneticist, who had emailed Roy explaining other chromosomal abnormalities that can be associated with ectopia cordis.

I saw how the information was lining up in Roy's head. The survival rate was negligible. There might be other chromosomal defects. The long-term prognosis was poor. If we pursued surgery we would potentially be bringing a baby into the world to experience a life of anaesthesia, operating tables, drips, needles and intensive care. And we would be entering that world ourselves.

'Yes, but what about what Father Lyons said?' I said. 'He thought our baby would still prefer a brief life, rather than no life at all.'

Roy looked unconvinced. While I was away he had spent an evening with a German friend, Frank, who was raised a Catholic. Frank is gay and when he was young the church's counsel had left him confused and ashamed. He warned Roy against following Catholic doctrines, pointing to the child abuse and other atrocities committed by church clergy.

Although Roy and I listened to each other and didn't shoot down each other's views, I began to wonder how we would find consensus.

The next day my mother called to tell me about Vicki Culling, a woman she had met at a midwifery council meeting. Vicki had written a book for couples facing a decision like ours – to continue or end a pregnancy in the face of an abnormal diagnosis. Vicki lived in Wellington and had offered to drop off a copy of the book. I met her on the street outside my office. As cars whizzed by, she told me that many years earlier she had lost a baby herself. She now volunteered for an organisation called Sands, which supported families when a baby died. Her book was called *Holding On & Letting Go*. She was surprised we hadn't been offered a copy at the hospital as she had secured a grant that meant they had a free supply. I found tears welling in my eyes. It was clear Vicki knew what we were going through and really cared.

Afterwards I found a note inside the book. 'I'm so sorry you even need to read this book. Please feel free to ring or email me at any time if you have any questions, no matter how small. We've supported many families who have been faced with the heartbreaking decision of when their baby lives or dies. As the book says, it's always about love. Hold on to that.'

I felt lucky that this book had arrived in my hands, although I discovered it was not an easy read. Reading about how the foetus looked after termination, the song played at the funeral, what the dead baby was dressed in – the stories had me in floods of tears. It was so close to what we could face ourselves. The full description of the termination procedure post-fourteen weeks left me aghast. The maternal foetal medicine team had glossed over the details when we met them. I learned that over forty-eight hours I would take two doses of a pill to stop pregnancy hormones. I would then be admitted to hospital to go into early labour. Like any birth, there would be contractions and pain. The foetus might show brief signs of life after being born.

Yet the book remained neutral on the best course of action. The woman who chose to end her pregnancy was not cold-hearted, it implied. The woman who continued, knowing her baby would die, was not a martyr.

We were hanging out to hear from Starship Hospital whether they would be willing to attempt surgery. By the time of our second appointment with the maternal foetal medicine team there was no news. Dr D was apologetic. She had written a letter and emailed, but there had been no response to date. The results of my blood-screening tests had showed a very low risk of the baby having any other chromosomal abnormality.

We had a list of other questions.

'What is the best way to make contact with a hospital overseas if surgery isn't possible in New Zealand?'

'Auckland may be able to refer you.'

'What is the cut-off date for termination?'

'Twenty weeks.'

Dr D had given us a report with all the measurements taken by the sonographer: biparietal diameter, femur length, head circumference, abdominal circumference, foetal weight. The measurements were plotted on a scale showing how our baby's growth compared with the national average. I could see he was well above average in all categories.

'Why is our baby growing so well with the heart he has?' I asked.

'Babies don't have to breathe in the womb,' she said. 'He's getting oxygen via the umbilical cord. It's when he's born and his lungs begin working and his heart has to pump oxygenated blood around his body that he'll have problems.'

After the appointment I felt none the wiser about anything. It felt as though we were getting nowhere.

'I think this baby has come from a distant dimension and is vibrating at a higher frequency than us. It's his first time incarnating in this world and fusing his soul with the body caused him problems.' Surendra wore wire-rimmed spectacles and had fine tawny blonde hair pulled back into a ponytail. I'd made a Skype appointment with the Dutch energy healer and seer, feeling I needed advice from someone who spent time thinking about souls and unseen dimensions.

On the screen of my computer I watched Surendra close his eyes and inhale slowly. 'Align your heart with the baby's heart. That is how you'll learn what it is he has come to show you. He may teach you about new ways of loving. The baby's soul is aware of the difficulty of the predicament. He may also choose to leave this life himself.'

The idea that the choice about our baby's life didn't simply rest on our shoulders, that the baby was making decisions too, was reassuring.

'Communicate with the baby and be open to the responses you might hear,' Surendra went on. 'If you choose to terminate, he will have a life on another plane, incarnate to other parents, or wait and incarnate to you. Also, miracles can happen if you and the baby fully commit to the realignment necessary for him to live.'

I neither believed nor disbelieved what Surendra said, but I was grateful he was offering me a story. A story to understand our situation was what I needed.

Two days later I visited a homeopath. Julie's home overlooked the sea. Aloe vera plants lined the path to her door. A crystal lamp glowed on her desk.

Julie was short and compact with bright eyes. 'Tell me everything that's happened, from the beginning,' she said. She took copious notes. When I finished talking she began testing for a homeopathic remedy. She had me place cards on my stomach, one by one, from a large stack. The cards were faced down so I couldn't see what was written on them. Julie noted the response from my muscles to gauge whether a card carried the name of a remedy I needed. The pile of twenty-five cards was whittled down to three, and then to one.

She turned over the last card. It listed mother's milk, amniotic fluid and oestrogen. I was stunned: the other cards in the pack had remedies from plants, flowers, metals and herbs. I touched each of the remedies on my card and tested positively for 'umbilical cord'.

Julie consulted one of her books to find out about this remedy. 'It is for children in danger,' she said. 'Information passes from mother to child via the umbilical cord. This remedy will help you connect and nourish your baby and vice versa.'

My appointment with Julie lasted nearly two hours. At the end she embraced me and asked me to stay in touch. I walked down her steps thinking what a privilege it had been to be in the hands of a healer so committed to her work. It felt as though people were appearing to hold our hands – Father Lyons, Vicki, Surendra, Julie. Meanwhile, though, Roy was engrossed in statistics about the unlikelihood of our baby's survival, and the fear that he would suffer after birth. By the end of the week our views were moving further and further apart. Inside I was beginning to quietly despair. One of us needed to shift perspective.

15 weeks

I pushed the phone so hard against my head my ear began to tingle. Dr D had news from Auckland. 'In principle they've said they would be willing to perform surgery on your baby's heart,' she reported.

'Really? Wow.' I was at work and had slipped into an empty meeting room.

'We'll fly you up for an appointment with their paediatric cardiologist, who will do an echocardiogram scan to look at his heart.'

'When?'

'Sometime in the next fortnight. Our administrator will be in touch with the booking details.'

'Thank you, Dr D. Thank you.'

I couldn't believe it. *They would be willing to perform surgery on your baby's heart.* I dialled Roy's number, already talking to him in my head. His phone switched to answerphone. It didn't matter – I would see him at home.

I went back to my desk, light-headed, amazed. Our baby might be one of those miracle wonder kids, the kind you hear about surviving when nobody thought they would. This was a scenario we'd barely dared to dream about.

Later in the day there was another surprise: a Facebook message from Ashley Monique Cardenas. She was the mother of Audrina, the toddler we'd seen on YouTube wearing pink plastic armour to shield her chest after her ectopia cordis heart had been successfully operated on in Texas.

'Hello Emma,' Ashley wrote. 'I'm so sorry to hear about ur baby boy. It's hard to hear the Drs state that there is nothing to do besides terminate ur pregnancy. Audrina is doing quite well and if I woulda terminated we wouldn't never know what a blessing she would be. Every situation is different and I'm willing to answer any questions I can for u. I hope u have a blessed day.'

I'd looked up Ashley on Facebook and messaged her, unsure whether I'd get a response. I was very grateful she'd replied to a stranger on the other side of the world. Ashley's message plus the news that we had an appointment in Auckland with the paediatric cardiologist left me feeling hopeful and buoyant.

That night I cooked chicken enchiladas with green sauce. I looked forward to eating them with Roy and regaling him with the day's developments. Seven o'clock passed, then eight o'clock and nine o'clock. I resisted the urge to call him. He had recently promised to forewarn me any night he was not going to be home for dinner. He was teaching four tutorials this semester and also had to submit his PhD proposal. I knew he was under pressure but my sympathy was spent. He arrived home after I'd gone to bed fuming.

When I told him the news from Auckland next morning, he was surprised but circumspect. 'If surgery is possible we still have to find out the chances of success and the long-term prognosis. Remember what Alix said.'

'I know, but at least we have some hope now.'

Carolyn wore high heels that make me think of Dr Seuss illustrations. They were black patent leather, with white leather at the front and talons that flared out like hooves. The counsellor's bright blonde hair and orange shirt matched her flamboyance.

'I know we're only supposed to work through the termination option with you,' I began. This was the impression I'd got when we'd asked the hospital for a referral to its counselling service.

'No, this space is for you to talk about whatever you need to,' Carolyn said.

We stated our positions. We didn't say anything we hadn't already said to each other. Roy spoke about not wanting the baby to have a short life of pain and distress. I spoke about my feeling it would be a greater act of love to bear with our baby until the end or give him the chance of life through surgery.

'How about we put both of your thoughts and feelings in a table? The good and not so good things about continuing or stopping the pregnancy.'

Carolyn began writing on a whiteboard. I liked her pragmatism. She asked us to think about which of our thoughts and feelings we were most attached to and which we were willing to compromise on. The idea that we could tease out the elements of our different perspectives offered hope we could find things to agree on. However, we didn't yet know how our appointment with the paediatric cardiologist in Auckland would influence our views.

Carolyn lent us a book, *The Prenatal Bombshell: Help and Hope When Continuing or Ending a Pregnancy after an Abnormal Diagnosis*, and encouraged us to make another appointment to see her.

The autumn sun was pale, like watered-down cordial, but it was still pleasant pedalling along the waterfront. We were going to be late for mass but I'd decided not to care. It was better to enjoy this moment with Roy. He rode his thin-wheeled road bike with the same grace and agility he danced salsa. When we hit the hill I struggled and had to get off and push.

As we entered the church we looked for an empty pew we could get to with minimal disruption. Father Lyons had just begun his homily. 'Motherhood is a very high calling. What relationship can ever replace the love of a mother and a grandmother? It is essential for women to realise that the love, guidance and influence they provide to their children are distinct and invaluable.'

It was Mother's Day. As at Easter, we had arrived at a service that seemed pertinent by accident rather than any conscious effort.

'In the light of Mary', Father Lyons continued, 'the church sees in the face of women the reflection of a beauty which mirrors the loftiest sentiments of which the human heart is capable: the self-offering totality of love; the strength that is capable of bearing the greatest sorrows.'

Again, I found myself sitting through most of the mass in tears. When we greeted Father Lyons afterwards he reminded us that the paediatric surgeon in his congregation would be happy to meet with us.

Later that afternoon, as Roy and I sat talking on the couch, he told me about a dream he'd had. He was walking with his nephew Adriano along the waterfront at Miraflores in Lima. They came across a market where there was a stall selling lollies. Roy told Adriano he could choose whatever he wanted. Adriano pointed to some sweets in a jar on a high shelf. Roy lifted him up to reach the jar. In that moment he felt overwhelmed with sadness at the thought he would never be able to lift our son up to reach a jar in a lolly shop. Then Adriano turned around. But it wasn't Adriano, it was our son. He put his arms around Roy and said, 'Don't worry, Papa, it's all right.'

I had tears in my eyes by the time Roy finished the story. It was a relief to hear him talk about a dream rather than cold facts. I believed Roy had received a message, from his own subconscious if nowhere else. I held his hand tightly and felt a togetherness that had been eluding us.

16 weeks

One night I felt little beats against the tight drumskin of my stomach. 'Is that you, baby?' The beats came again. Knock, knock, knock. It was a thrilling conversation.

Every morning that week something strange had happened: each time I woke up my stomach had swollen to a bigger size. Of course, you might say, I was pregnant – what did I expect? That was true, but it didn't make the changes feel any less peculiar.

My baby's kicks, my tummy's expansion – these things were special, yet bittersweet because of the possibility they might not continue. We had taken a pause in our decision-making until after the appointment with the paediatric cardiologist in Auckland. A date still hadn't been confirmed for this and I'd begun to feel anxious about the timing. At the end of this week there would be just three weeks before the cut-off point for termination. At my request, the maternal foetal medicine unit in Wellington phoned Auckland Hospital. It turned out the hospital needed to wait until I was eighteen weeks pregnant so they could get a better view of the baby's heart and anatomy. They would schedule an appointment for the week after next. This meant Roy and I would have just a few days to make our final decision. If we decided to end the pregnancy it would have to happen the following week. By then I would be nineteen weeks pregnant.

'Is it okay if we just stay for an hour?' I asked Roy as we drove to a Latino potluck dinner on Saturday night.

'I don't know, Emma. Let's see how it goes.'

'But we have to drive to Paekākāriki afterwards. I don't want to leave too late.' We were going to spend the night with Thomasin and her partner Stephen in their family bach, about a forty-minute drive away.

'Everything has to be your way, doesn't it?' Roy said.

I didn't want to go to the potluck. It was a frenetic Peruvian Zumba teacher's birthday. She was prone to making everyone who entered her house dance, whether they wanted to or not.

'Sometimes you're so controlling,' Roy continued.

'You're the one being selfish,' I said. 'Maybe if you could drive you'd understand.' Roy still hadn't learned to drive, despite his promises and frequent encouragement from me.

We'd been fractious with each other all week. I didn't want to nag, but things like dirty dishes never seemed to get done otherwise. I knew that in the big picture dishes weren't a big deal, but in the context of day-to-day living they mattered. Our spats scared me. Were they a sign we were flawed as a couple?

What we were not arguing about was the big gap between our views on what to do about our baby. We were both acutely aware of this gap but neither of us knew how to bridge it. Perhaps that was where the tension was really coming from.

We stayed at the dinner an hour and a half. Civil chit-chat with strangers cooled us down but I was still upset, and as we drove to Paekākāriki I wanted to talk more. It was classic male–female behaviour. I wanted to express emotion and be heard. Roy wanted to move past the emotion into solving the problem. If we weren't solving a problem, what, he thought, was the point of the conversation?

Next day we raced back to Wellington for another round of open homes. The pressure was on to buy a house or secure another rental.

The house we were renting was likely to be demolished in a month, and two weeks later Roy was leaving for a conference in Mexico and a trip to Peru to see his family. He would be gone two months. The trip had been booked back in February, before we'd got our baby's diagnosis. He'd looked into shortening it but the cost of changing flights had been exorbitant.

There was a cream weatherboard cottage with maroon windowsills I'd liked on Adelaide Road in Newtown. By the time I'd talked myself into living on a road with heavy traffic, the GV of $415,000 had shot up to $480,000, out of our range. There was another cottage on Adelaide Road I liked, but at the open home we learned it was already under offer. A nice light house in Northland was way off the beaten track and already swarming with people when we got to the open home. A Petone cottage, 'buyer enquiry over $380,000', was a good price but cold and dark. An Island Bay house was going for a song and had sea views but needed serious re-piling work. That Sunday we also saw a Melrose place with no sun, a nice Brooklyn cottage on an incessantly busy road, and a run-down student flat in Wilton that smelled of mould.

The pattern of hopes raised by alluring pictures and jaunty descriptions on real estate websites and hopes dashed when we discovered the house was a dive, or out of our price range, or already sold, was becoming more and more tiring. We were like wind-up toys, zigzagging around the city, arguing about whether we needed to turn on GPS for directions, rushing to make it in time for the tail end of a half-hour open home. By the end of the day we were deflated and cross with each other. The chances of us finding, buying and moving into a house in the next six weeks seemed remote. Not knowing where we were going to live added to the stress we were already feeling.

17 weeks

'The chances of surgery being successful may be small but they are not zero, and as long as they are not zero there is hope.' Brendon Bowkett, the paediatric surgeon, was short and burly with light blonde hair. He talked quickly and concisely, as if he already had a diagram in his head illustrating the points he wanted to cover.

It was four-thirty on a Friday afternoon and we were sitting in his office in Wellington Hospital. He had been in theatre that day and I imagined he'd usually be knocking off about now. Our private meeting with him had been orchestrated by Father Lyons. Our Auckland appointment was scheduled for Monday so seeing him was well-timed: I hoped he would equip us with the right questions to ask.

That week I'd been reading *The Wet Engine* by Brian Doyle. The book was in part homage to a young paediatric cardiologist who'd performed heart surgery to save the life of one of the author's twin babies. It had slipped into my hands at just the right moment thanks to Emily, a woman in my writing group. A small purple hardcover, the book was full of beautiful musings. The heart, Doyle wrote, was the first organ to form. It pulsed from when the baby was about twenty days old but no one knew exactly what caused the heart's cells to begin beating in unison. In an average lifetime the heart would beat two billion times.

We discovered Brendon already knew quite a lot about our baby as he'd looked at the hospital file. He began drawing some of the surgical options on a piece of foolscap paper. Creating a cavity for the heart to nestle within would be one of the main challenges, but a piece of baby's lung could potentially be removed to make room. Lungs could grow back in babies, apparently. Or if there was already space for baby's heart to sit partially inside his chest then skin could be stretched over the top to protect it.

'Babies still have such pliable skin,' he said.

It was if we were talking with an architect about how to remodel a room, or a car mechanic keen to show what could be done to fix an engine.

'If things go well with surgery there's a high chance the baby could live a very normal life afterwards. I wouldn't expect high morbidity,' he continued. 'It's usually in the six hours or so after birth that a baby will declare itself as being a candidate for surgery or not.

'I want to emphasise that any baby's comfort is our primary concern, so we do everything we can to ensure this. Your baby won't suffer, I assure you.'

The question of our baby's suffering had been one of the key planks in Roy's argument that surgery might not be a good idea. It was if Brendon already knew the fears we had and planned to dispel them.

He told us that much more common than ectopia cordis is a condition called pentalogy of Cantrell, in which the intestines or other organs spill outside a baby's abdomen. 'We operate on these here with about a ninety-eight percent success rate. Babies can be out of hospital in a few weeks.'

To illustrate his point he offered to take us to the neonatal ward, where a baby on whom he had operated three days earlier was recovering. He was keen for us see the ward was not all beeping machines, red flashing lights and hushed tension.

There were four babies in incubators and one propped up in what looked like a baby car seat. The parents of the baby the doctor had brought us to see were teenagers. Sitting next to their baby girl, they looked shell-shocked but calm. Inside the incubator their baby was gazing around placidly, looking like any other newborn. I wanted to stay longer, but it seemed rude to invade the couple's space.

Brendon took us back out into the beige hospital corridor. He knew about our appointment in Auckland and told us that, while we should be guided by that team, he would be willing to operate on our baby provided his heart had no other defects.

'But how would you know the best way to proceed?' Roy said. 'This condition is so rare there are few studies.'

'It's true that these kinds of surgeries are so rare we have to do things on the fly. We often do things we've never done before,' the doctor said.

This meeting had been a revelation, the only taste of optimism from a health professional we'd had since our baby's diagnosis. I could tell the experience had moved Roy, shifted things around in his mind. He thought the doctor's take might be overly optimistic, but I heard him later excitedly telling his friend Javier on the phone about our visit to the neonatal ward and how babies' lungs can grow back.

18 weeks

Regina Spektor's song 'Fidelity' filled the cabin as our plane took off. I loved this song. Way back in the beginning of our relationship, Roy and I had danced to it in my lounge at one a.m. with the lights turned down low, drunk on red wine. At the time the song had spoken to me about myself, the single thirty-something who'd had plenty of flings but whose relationships had inevitably flopped. How different things were now. I was sitting next to a man I loved fully. Inside me was our baby boy, who had brought about a new kind of intense, wondrous love unlike anything I'd felt before. My eyes filled with tears as the plane surged upwards. I was happy. I was grateful for the love in my life and the way it coloured everything more brightly, filling in pockets of loneliness I hadn't even realised were there.

I was optimistic about the appointment in Auckland. Our meeting with Brendon Bowkett had brought about a sea change. Roy and I now both felt surgery was worth a shot.

Auckland Hospital was a disjointed collection of buildings, some bordering a motorway. It seemed unlikely that feats of healing could take place within such a mess of ramps and aluminium windows and perplexing signs. The maternal foetal medicine clinic was much bigger than Wellington's and the waiting room was packed with a cross-section of Aucklanders. A young Asian couple sat tapping their smartphones. Two Pacific Island women opened lunchboxes and unwrapped sandwiches for three small children. A rotund woman was wearing a pink tracksuit adorned with sequined bunny faces. I wondered about the stories in the room. The general air of boredom belied the serious reasons that had caused us all to trek here.

Finally we met paediatric cardiologist Dr Gentles. A small man with gnome-white hair, he suited his name. He performed a scan – an ultrasound just like the ones I'd had before – zooming in on the heart to look at its structure. I couldn't decipher anything from the pulsating swirls on the screen. Dr Gentles said little. Afterwards we waited in the appointment room, Roy's arm around my shoulders, until he came to deliver the findings.

'There are two issues with your baby's heart,' he reported. 'One is its position outside the chest. The other is the anatomy of the heart itself. There are defects.'

He produced a photocopied diagram of a heart and drew on it to illustrate the anatomical problems. 'One of the ventricles is smaller than the other and there is a hole between the two that shouldn't be there,' he explained. 'The aortic valve that carries oxygen-rich blood from the heart to the body is much smaller than it should be.' I concentrated hard on the diagrams and his words.

'Sometimes we see hearts like this inside a baby's chest and we can offer a series of surgeries, although the life expectancy is still reduced. But your baby also has ectopia cordis and his heart is not just partly outside his chest but a long way. The pentacles attaching his heart to his insides can't just be squashed back inside the chest.'

'So what does that mean?' I said.

'Your baby is not a candidate for surgery. If you continued the pregnancy he would be likely to die at birth or shortly after, if he makes it to full term.'

'How would he die?' asked Roy.

'He may die of asphyxiation or–'

'Do you mean he won't be able to breathe?'

'No, possibly not.'

This was not the news I'd been expecting to hear. I thought my baby's heart was fine. It was just in the wrong place. I thought we had the chance for some miracle surgery. I was surprised. There were two problems with his heart. The sum total made his death an inevitability. I was calm for most of the time the doctor was speaking, then I broke down into tears I couldn't stop.

We left the hospital exhausted and disorientated. Almost immediately I noticed the idea of a termination sat differently in my head. If there was a chance my baby could live I would've fought for him. Now there was no chance. Our baby was not going to be one of those miracle kids who survived when nobody thought they would. The farewell was a forgone conclusion. Was there any point in postponing this?

It was dusk by the time we got to my mother's house, where we were staying the night. Although an icy winter wind was blowing I wanted to walk down to the beach to see the sea, inhale the salt. Once there, Roy and I huddled together on a wooden bench. Rangitoto Island was a lump of black coal on the horizon.

Much later I would research my son's heart defects. First, though, I asked myself if I wanted to know the details: becoming cognisant might feel like watching a car crash being replayed in slow motion. It would also prove difficult to get to grips with the unfamiliar language of heart anatomy, words like foramen ovale, pulmonary artery and ductus arteriosus.

The American Heart Association's website had a large section devoted to heart defects. I carefully read the fact sheet about hypoplastic left heart syndrome, the name Dr Gentles had given to our baby's other condition. The fact sheet said a healthy heart took in oxygen-poor blood, pumped the blood into the lungs where it was oxygenated, then pumped the oxygen-rich blood back out into the body. I imagined the red blood cells as waiters, carrying trays of oxygen to hungry muscles, tissues and organs. When their trays were empty they returned to the heart for replenishment.

With hypoplastic left heart syndrome the left side of the heart is critically underdeveloped and unable properly to do its job of receiving oxygen from the lungs and pumping it back into the body. Without surgery, the condition is fatal. This, together with ectopia cordis, added up to a list of problems too complex for a surgeon to attempt to fix.

Back home in Wellington the information from Dr Gentles became the new norm to live with. Our darling boy was going to die. There was no hope for him. One way or another we would have to say goodbye.

I was struggling, searching for something to make his life still a good thing. I wanted to latch on to one bright thought, a speck of glitter, to make the situation bearable. I realised that the idea of fighting for even a slim chance of my son's survival and doing right by him as his mother had been a major force in my thinking. And without that – well, was there any point? Grief now or grief later, what was the difference? Maybe it was better to let go now. I feared that the rest of my pregnancy would be a sad slow mourning, followed by the fanfare and palaver of a funeral, of everyone knowing we had lost a baby. Did we want that? The full-blown version of grief and public ritual sounded exhausting.

Roy and I headed out for a walk along Oriental Parade. It was just after sunset and the sky was fast being scribbled over by winter's darkness. We came across a wooden seat, facing the sea, that had small bouquets of flowers attached at either end. Plastic butterflies fluttered among daisies, violets and pansies. Sitting underneath the bouquets were two plastic octopuses wielding samurai swords – children's toys. A bronze plaque attached to the seat explained this tableau.

Our Su-Yen, gone ahead to the arms of Jesus
See you at the end of the beach darling
Our love forever… Mum & Dad
Su-Yen Bok (2004 – 2013)

'She liked butterflies,' said a woman who had appeared at the seat.
'It's a lovely tribute,' I said, my chin trembling. 'Did you know her?'
The woman explained she had been Su-Yen's teacher. The little girl had died in a sudden accident. These flowers marked the one-year anniversary of her death. The teacher was taking a photo to share with Su-Yen's class.

Roy had seen an abandoned child's woollen hat with a pom-pom earlier on our walk. He went and fetched it and placed it on Su-Yen's seat in case she was cold on this winter night.

I didn't want it to seem to the teacher that we were grief tourists, so I told her we were going to lose a baby.

'Ah, I'm sorry, I've been there too. I wish you all the best,' she said. I could tell by her eyes she meant it. In that moment, standing with a stranger on a winter's night, observing a tribute to a girl we'd never met, it felt as though we were members of a group, united by the shared experience of losing children. The words on the plaque, 'See you at the end of the beach darling', went straight to my heart. I imagined the parents coming to Oriental Bay with their daughter, paddling on the beach, buying gelato from the shop at the end. Woven into the words were the parents' mourning, memory, love and longing to see their daughter again. *See you at the end of the beach darling.*

When I went to work next day, my mind kept playing images of delivering a dead foetus, holding a funeral. Tears leaked from my eyes. Was this what grief was like, the bottomless feeling I'd heard described? It felt incongruous that our little boy was still so active. He kicked and wriggled inside me. The rest of his body was growing as it should. He was flourishing except for the one crucial fact: his heart was blooming out from his chest like a flower attached to a stem.

At my desk, I made the mistake of opening an electronic brochure on late-term terminations emailed to me by the midwife at the hospital. I'd rung the day before, wanting to know exactly how long we had to make our decision. I knew the hospital performed terminations only up to twenty weeks, unless it had special legal consent. How far before the twenty-week mark would we have to book in? Did the procedure, which would take several days, have to be finished by the time you reached twenty weeks, or just begun at twenty weeks? These timings would dictate how much time we had and time felt crucial.

I didn't get the clear answers I was hoping for. The midwife who rang back after I'd left a message was not Louise but Kris, who was filling in while Louise was on three weeks' annual leave. I felt angry and confused. Why hadn't Louise mentioned she was going away when we'd spoken a few days earlier? Now I would need to explain our situation to a new midwife.

The brochure was very matter-of-fact.

Preparing for the birth of your baby
Your labour will be induced. A Mifegyne tablet will be given 48 hours before you are admitted to hospital. Once you are admitted to hospital Misoprostol tablets will be used to soften the cervix and start the contractions. A further brochure with details and contact information will be given to you when the medication is commenced.

You usually remain in the same room throughout your labour, baby's birth, and until you go home. You may wish to bring things you find comforting e.g. personal family photos with you into hospital. Your partner/support person is able to stay and support you for the duration of labour and birth. Do not be afraid to ask for help from hospital staff, and to accept offers of support.

If your pregnancy is over 23 weeks you would need to labour on Delivery Suite. Your baby is usually stillborn. Sometimes babies can show some signs of life, e.g. a weak heartbeat and some small reflex movements. In this situation we would normally wrap baby to keep him/her warm and very soon the baby's heartbeat will stop.

Your baby will have very little body fat and his/her skin may look quite red and translucent. There may be some bruising caused by the delivery. In reality the abnormalities are quite often less than you have imagined. Your baby may look perfect.

Your milk may 'come in' a few days after baby's birth. This can be painful but wearing a firm fitting bra and taking pain relief as needed will help. Tablets to suppress lactation can be prescribed and should be started within 24 hours of delivery.

Occasionally not all the placenta is delivered after your baby's birth. A D&C (Dilation and Curettage) operation is then advised to avoid infection. This is a brief operation performed under general anaesthetic.

You will be offered a post-mortem of your baby. There is a post-mortem brochure 'PANUI for post-mortem exam (PMMRC)' available for you to read and keep.

Legal Requirements

If your baby is stillborn before 20 weeks of pregnancy and weighs less than 400 grams the baby's birth is not registered, and there is no legal requirement to bury him/her, although you are able to have a funeral if you wish. If you do not wish to arrange a funeral yourself, the cremation of your baby can be arranged by the hospital. This service is free.

I sat at my desk reading the brochure with tears spilling down my cheeks, hoping no colleague was about to tap me on the shoulder and ask me something.

19 weeks

Since we got back from Auckland questions had begun arising again. I was groping around, trying to get a sense of the way forward. What would be the story we'd want to tell in years to come? Would it be comforting to know our baby had decided when to exit? Would we be left with a feeling of blood on our hands if we made the decision on his behalf? Or would we be setting ourselves and him free by facing the facts and not postponing his end? Where did the greatest opportunity for love lie?

The termination process sounded awful. That much was clear. If I went through with it I would be going against my body's maternal instincts. A massive dose of hormones would suddenly, abruptly, undo everything. I didn't know how we could honour the little foetus we'd be left with at the end. Who would meet the barely formed baby? I couldn't imagine holding a funeral but how would we create a fitting farewell? My mother would be at a conference in Prague at the time. I could think of only a few other people with whom I'd feel comfortable to share the experience. A few weeks later Roy would be leaving for his two months in South America. I would be alone to face grief through the middle of winter.

Are we heartless if we terminate? Foolish if we continue? What's the best way for me to mother my baby? Where do the signs seem to be leading? What path offers the most growth and learning? I was searching for a question to supersede all the others, one whose answer would lead to a eureka moment when I'd finally know what to do. But there were so many questions and no right or wrong answers. I realised I could go on searching forever but a perfect answer didn't exist. Either way was a leap in the dark. Either way there would be heartache.

Roy and I decided to go away for the weekend to make our final decision. Stephen and Thomasin had lent us their family bach. By the time we were on State Highway One I was pretty certain I knew what I wanted to do. I just wasn't sure if Roy would agree.

Next morning we walked along Paekākāriki Beach, inhaling salty air, picking our way among driftwood. The sky was breathtakingly blue and the sun unusually hot for late autumn.

When we reached the end of the beach we sat in the sand, leaning against big rocks. I told Roy about a phone conversation I'd had with Vicki Culling. I'd cut to the chase with the question I most wanted to ask. 'Do you think women who have terminations find the emotional process easier? Is the grief less than for women who continue pregnancies knowing their baby is going die?'

Vicki had drawn a breath and begun with a caveat. 'There is not a one-size-fits-all answer. So much depends on the individual woman and her circumstances. That said, I don't think grief is any less one way or the other. In some cases I've seen massive guilt and self-judgement arise in women who've chosen terminations, even though they felt their decision was rational. On the other hand, in some cases I've seen a sense of peace in women who have continued pregnancies and farewelled babies after their birth – maybe because they were able to make good memories with their babies through the pregnancy, and in the things they did after baby had passed.'

Vicki said it could be hard for friends and family to share in the grief and offer support after a termination, hard to comprehend the experience without baby photos or a casket.

Vicki's words validated many of the hunches I'd been having but I'd sensed an unspoken expectation in some family members and friends that I would terminate. Vicki had been at pains to emphasise that Sands supported families whatever decision they made. For some, she said, terminating was the right thing to do.

Roy listened quietly, then he said, 'But Emsy, we know our son is going to die and we have to face that. If we continue the pregnancy it's going to mean suffering for him when he's born. He'll die of suffocation.

I don't want to do that to him. I don't want to have to watch that.'

'How do you know his soul wouldn't choose to have that brief experience of living though? Maybe for reasons we can't understand it's important to let nature take its course.'

'If you're talking about souls you're talking about mysteries we can never hope to understand. We're his parents and as parents you must make choices, even if they are hard choices. We are going to have to let him go and it will be easier to do that sooner rather than later.'

We didn't raise our voices through this conversation. We were willing to hear each other's arguments again. While we were talking I'd absent-mindedly drawn an outline of a heart in the sand and filled it with pebbles and fragments of driftwood. Roy, meanwhile, had made a small cone-shaped mountain with a seagull feather stuck on the top.

'Look,' he said, gesturing towards our creations. 'You are thinking with your heart and emotion. I'm trying to view the situation more objectively, from the top of a mountain.' I thought it was arrogant of Roy to claim his perspective was more objective than mine but I didn't say so. I dearly hoped my heart and his mountain would find a way to merge.

We didn't talk more about the decision that afternoon. We set off to Waikanae, a town further up the coast where my grandmother had lived for many years, and stopped on the way for ice creams. We drove by the three different houses my grandmother had owned. We walked along the beach among a throng of kids, dogs, couples and teenagers until sunset painted the sky. Without saying so, I think we both sensed the need to rest and unwind and find a little happiness together, to be a carefree couple again.

Afterwards Roy wanted to go for dinner at the Fisherman's Table, a family restaurant serving big portions and an all-you-can-eat salad bar. I usually turned my nose up at this kind of food, but I acquiesced. We bantered convivially about Roy's PhD supervisors, the annual report I'd soon have to begin writing, what Roy was going to do in Peru, the love life of his friend Nacho.

When we arrived back at the house, an orange crescent moon was slowly sinking towards the inky black sea. We stood watching the magical sight and out of nowhere Roy said, 'Maybe we just have to wait for our son to go in his own time like the moon. Maybe we should bear with him.'

I was amazed to hear him say these words. 'Yes,' I said, hugging him tightly.

Next morning the glorious weather held. After breakfast we walked on the beach again. Despite what Roy had said the night before, his point of view had not really changed. We stepped gingerly around the subject, wary of conflict. We wished we could stay longer in Paekākāriki, perhaps to postpone the moment when one of us would have to concede. So many times I'd said to my friends and family, 'We have a fifty-fifty part in making this baby. If either of us feels forced or coerced into doing something we don't want to do, it will create trouble in our future. How will we be able to love each other through the next hard stage if one of us resents the choice that's been made? We need to find consensus.'

Cleaning the house that afternoon was beset with difficulties. While I was washing the sheets, the spin cycle of the washing machine broke down and the machine was full of water that wouldn't empty. That morning the shower head had come off in Roy's hand. I was worried we were leaving a trail of destruction. It was sunset by the time we finished and had packed our things, but we still hadn't decided. We sat together on the deck. Crunch time was here.

'I want to continue the pregnancy but I won't do it without your support,' I said.

'I think it's best to have a termination,' Roy said.

Sobs shook my body. 'Don't make me do this, don't make me end our baby's life. I love him too much. What about what you said last night?'

'Okay fine,' Roy said, 'we'll do it your way. I can't make you have a termination. But you must promise me you won't spiral into depression after he dies. I don't know if you're going to recover from this.'

And then the conversation was over, maybe ten minutes after it began. It was now dark and time to leave. We didn't say much on the drive home. Roy seemed distant but I didn't want to force more talk.

Over the next days I replayed in my mind the moment on the deck at sunset when Roy switched from saying no to saying yes. I was keeping my baby but I didn't know what it was going to cost me in terms of my relationship. I tried to talk to Roy to find out how the choice was sitting, to get an emotional update. He closed down these enquiries. I couldn't tell if he was angry with me or simply didn't want to go through the painful conversation again. Without his reassurance, I worried that I was asking him to do something he might hate me for. Would the pregnancy put a wedge between us that we wouldn't recover from? I was scared.

My mind lurched about. Maybe a termination would be better? Maybe I was the foolish one? Even though I'd made the decision I was now second-guessing it. I talked to friends. Several conversations left me feeling emptier than beforehand. I was looking for reassurance my friends simply couldn't give.

One lunchtime when I was in the kitchen a colleague asked me how I was and I burst into tears. We shuffled into a meeting room. 'You know I had a stillborn baby,' she said. 'I think that even though continuing the pregnancy is a longer road, it might be easier to move on from than termination.'

I clung to her words. I knew I wanted to keep my baby. The hard bit was feeling guilty either way – guilt for terminating my beloved baby one way, guilt for making my beloved partner do something he didn't want to do the other way. How to resolve this? Friday was the absolute deadline if we wanted to reconsider the option of termination.

Roy suggested we see Carolyn again. Due to a cancellation we were able to get an appointment on the Friday. Carolyn heard us out. 'Both of your perspectives are valid,' she said. 'There is no right or wrong answer. But one of you will have to make a compromise and the question is for whom will the compromise be harder? Who has the most to lose?'

Gently, she suggested the stakes might be higher for me since it was my body that would bear the brunt of the decision. 'The risk is that you'll hate yourself and hate Roy if you end up having a termination you don't want. But Roy, you have rights too. And if you are making this compromise, what other ways can your needs be met? What would you like to have control over during the pregnancy and birth?'

'Well, I'd like to be sure our son is not in pain when he's born and I'd like him to be baptised.'

I could see Roy respected Carolyn's logic. Compromising didn't mean he had to believe that my reasoning was better than his. It didn't mean I was right and he was wrong.

'It's important to know that you're not going to be angry with me during the pregnancy,' I said.

'I'm not angry, Emma. I need to support you in this decision.'

We left the appointment with a firm resolve to continue the pregnancy and I knew I now had Roy's blessing. I was relieved, elated. We went to a restaurant for lunch and held hands across the table. It felt like a celebration. That afternoon I wrote a list of people to whom we'd tell the news. It felt like a happy announcement. I was keeping my baby.

I phoned my mother in Prague to let her know. It was early summer there and I could hear a bird twittering as we spoke. She said if she had been in my shoes she would probably have made the same decision. This meant a lot to me.

20 weeks

'I have a gift for you.' Father Lyons produced a small white box from his pocket. Roy and I had made another appointment to see the priest and this time we'd been ushered into the vicarage where he lived. I'd emailed beforehand and told him about the specialist's verdict in Auckland. He seemed genuinely saddened and told us he had visited the grave of Suzanne Aubert, the nun he wished canonised, to ask again for a miracle for our baby in her name.

Inside the white box was a silver saint's medallion on a chain. 'Have you heard of St Christopher?' he asked. We hadn't. He explained that he was a saint of the people, not recorded in scripture or beatified by the Vatican but loved and worshipped nonetheless. Settling back in his chair, his hands resting on his stomach, he told us the saint's story.

St Christopher, patron saint of travellers, became famous for saving the life of a baby during a great flood. To reach safety, Christopher had to cross a treacherous swollen river and he did so swimming with the baby on his back. As he was crossing the river he realised it was not him who was saving the baby's life, but the baby who was saving his, giving him the strength and determination to reach the other side when he might otherwise have given up. On reaching safety, the baby on his back disappeared. It is thought to have been the Christ Child.

'Perhaps, like Christopher, you too are carrying a Christ Child who will guide you to the other side of this difficult experience,' the priest said in his gentle melodious voice.

I loved this story, and the idea that in some intellect-defying way my son could actually be saving me. I was touched, too, by the gift of the medallion, which was etched with Saint Christopher wading through water and a haloed child on his shoulder pointing the way ahead. Father Lyons advised me to wear it on my person or keep it somewhere I could see it often. 'Your baby is very lucky to have you as parents,' he said.

Since we had made the decision to continue the pregnancy, my sense of peace had only increased. I hadn't had a single niggly doubt. Given my capacity for doubting much smaller decisions, this had surprised me. Was this because I had truly listened to my heart? I had been dabbling in heart research and had learned there's some physiological truth to this. Our heart rate changes with emotions and decision-making. The heart itself has around 40,000 neurons like those found in the brain. The emerging field of neurocardiology, is specifically interested in understanding how communication works between our hearts and minds.

When I thought of my baby all I felt was tenderness. Someone said to me it was brave act to continue the pregnancy, as if we were making a sacrifice, but all I wanted to do was love him and it was easy to go forward with that feeling.

Roy and I were getting on much better too. After the past weeks of conflict, he had softened again towards me and our baby. He caressed my stomach in bed at night, and in the morning gave his son kisses through my skin and made little jokes with him. He had also proposed a name for him: Jesús Valentino.

'No, we can't call our baby Jesús,' I'd said. Jesús – pronounced 'Hey-zeus' – is a common name in Spanish-speaking countries but I didn't think it'd translate well to New Zealand.

'But it's only fair. You get to choose one name and I get to choose one,' Roy said.

It was true that I'd suggested the name Valentino as I'd found out on Valentine's Day that I was pregnant. But I hadn't counted on Roy making Valentino part of an extravagant double-barrelled name. 'People will think we're calling our son the Messiah if we call him Jesús!' I protested.

Now my pregnancy had the green light, I had a lot to do. Rub oil on my stomach every morning to prevent stretch marks. Take iron pills twice a day. Do daily pelvic floor exercises, and leg elevations for my varicose veins. Go to pregnancy yoga once a week. Floss my teeth at night as my gums had started bleeding. Remember to talk to my baby. Do my Buddhist chanting every morning. Avoid processed foods, sushi and mayonnaise. Sleep only on my left side. My head started to spin. On a yellow Post-it note I wrote a list and stuck it on my mirror. I probably wouldn't do half these things but writing the list made me feel better.

There was another important matter to attend to. Although I had large breasts naturally, they had suddenly swelled to alarming proportions. Apparently this was due to my growing milk ducts. One lunch break I went into a lingerie shop to buy new bras. I'm usually a 12E so I picked a few 12Gs to try. Unfortunately, even with these bucket-sized cups I spilled out the sides.

'How are you getting on for size?' asked a sales assistant outside my fitting room.

'Um, I think this one is too small,' I said, pulling back the curtain.

'I think we should go to a 12H,' she said gravely.

'Gosh, I didn't even know you could get bras that big.'

'Well, we only carry two H-cup models in the store,' she admitted.

Great, I thought to myself, my breast size really was almost off the

Richter scale. When I tried the 12H I had to admit it was a good fit, but it was also very expensive. Special models didn't come cheap. The sales assistant then proposed 14G in two less expensive styles that might work. They did, luckily.

That night I sheepishly told Roy his girlfriend was now officially a G-cup.

'G for grande,' he said. He sounded quite chuffed. 'Can I post that on Facebook?'

That weekend, exactly halfway through my pregnancy, I had my first regular check-up with my midwife. Tessa came to our house and we chatted over cups of tea and slices of shortbread. She gave me a large blue appointment book, measured my stomach – which, as the baby was big, was the size you would expect a few weeks later in gestation – and listened to his heartbeat. As he was darting around it took a while to find it. 'Don't worry,' Tessa said, 'that's a good sign. It's the ones that don't move much you worry about. His heart rate is normal.'

She took my blood pressure, which was also fine. The focus of the maternal foetal medicine team had been on what was wrong with my baby, rather than the more mundane matter of my health and how the pregnancy was progressing. This dose of normality was nice.

'What do you think of the name Jesús Valentino for our son?' Roy asked Tessa. I rolled my eyes. In the face of my lack of enthusiasm, Roy had begun canvassing others for support.

'Ha! It's very distinctive. It's a good name,' Tessa said. I thought she and others were too polite to admit the name might be a little over the top.

As our appointment wrapped up I thanked Tessa for being willing to stay on board as our midwife and for supporting the decision we'd taken. I valued her inner calmness. She confessed that one of her colleagues had suggested she might want to leave our care in the hands of the hospital, given the difficulties and complexities of the pregnancy. 'But,' she said, 'I've thought you were an amazing couple from the first time I met you and I couldn't walk away now. It's a privilege to be asked to stand by you. Besides, I've got to stick around and find out if this baby ends up being called Jesús Valentino.'

21 weeks

I'd declared to the universe and a couple of bemused friends that I wanted to find a house to buy by the end of the weekend. That way there might be just enough time for the purchase before Roy left for Mexico and Peru in three weeks. The demolition of our rental had been postponed, but we still had to be out by the end of July, only six weeks away. We needed to find a new home, and we needed to find it fast.

If we couldn't, Plan B was to put our belongings into storage and for me to stay with a friend until Roy got back. Thomasin and another friend, Amy, had both offered to have me. While the idea of company appealed, I wasn't keen on living out of a suitcase with a baby on the way. Also, I'd be eight months pregnant by the time Roy returned – not a great time to be house-hunting under pressure, then unpacking and setting up a new home. The main problem with my grand plan of buying a house in the next three weeks was that after six months of looking we hadn't been able to find one. Still, in theory, our future house could be just around the corner.

After trawling through property websites, I remembered one more place to add to our list of open homes. It had only two bedrooms and might be on the expensive side but Roy liked the look of the photographs.

When we arrived at 6 Ariki Road, we couldn't see the house. A steep flight of steps disappeared into trees. As Roy pulled me up huffing and puffing, a white stucco 1940s house with a flat roof and grey-blue window shutters emerged. Enormous windows in the dining room and lounge framed views of the Remutaka Ranges, the southern part of the city and the harbour. This was the dividend for all those steps. Houses were reduced to the size of matchboxes, roads to grey shoelaces.

The rooms had a spacious feel, with white walls and polished wooden floors but the kitchen and bathroom were run-down, with peeling paint and old lino. 'The house has been rented for a decade or so and these rooms have suffered,' the real estate agent admitted.

'What do you think?' I said to Roy.

'I like it,' he said quietly.

'I like it too. I don't think it would be too hard to fix up the kitchen and bathroom.'

During our months of house-hunting, there had been only a few homes on which Roy and I had immediately agreed. It was a promising start. We continued our tour of open homes. A sold sign had been slapped on a property in Miramar. A 1980s house in a subdivision close to the airport did not appeal. A two-bedroom place in Brooklyn, the estate sale of a man who'd raised tropical fish in the basement, was already under offer. A great ex-state house in Strathmore was swarming with fifty hungry buyers. Hours later, 6 Ariki Road was still the most promising thing we'd seen. The real estate agent had promised to send us a builder's report and a Land Information Memorandum (LIM) report, both of which already existed. This boded well.

That week the physicality of pregnancy suddenly became very real. My insides felt like a box wedged with polystyrene packing, with no room for my organs to move. My legs felt heavy. Half my clothes didn't fit any more and my new look was oversized shirts over stretchy black pants. If it wasn't already obvious I was pregnant, it soon would be.

I needed to make the announcement to my work colleagues, none of whom knew except my manager, Sarah, who was also a good friend. I was nervous about how they'd react. At the end of one day, when the office had cleared out, I wrote an email explaining I was pregnant with a baby with a fatal heart condition. The next morning when I arrived at work I found an email from the chief executive encouraging me to take the day off. 'Let the dust settle if you don't want to face people,' she said.

I knew she meant to be supportive, but her suggestion made me feel a bit paranoid. Had my email been inappropriate? Was it too hard for people to hear about a baby that was not expected to survive? I realised that while I'd had two months to process the news, it was a shock for others to hear it. A few of my female colleagues who had children sent me thoughtful, sensitive emails. A couple were brave enough to come and give me teary hugs. But most who received my email said nothing. I could relate to what Elizabeth Tova Bailey wrote in her memoir about living with a mysterious illness that almost killed her: 'I was a reminder of all they feared: chance, uncertainty, loss and the sharp edge of mortality. Those of us with illnesses are the holders of the silent fears of those with good health'. Perhaps my baby's condition also represented people's silent fears.

That same day I went to a drop-in Buddhist meeting at lunchtime. The kaikan, a peaceful oasis in a high-rise building, was a centre for Nichiren Daishonin Buddhism, a branch of Mahayana Buddhism that originated in Japan in the thirteenth century. The central practice is to chant before an altar containing a scroll inscribed with an excerpt from Buddha's lotus sutra, the last sutra he wrote. The words chanted – 'Nam-myoho-renge-kyo' – are said to bring you into harmony with the universe and the laws of cause and effect, and help you manifest your potential for Buddhahood.

I was first introduced to Nichiren Buddhism when I was nineteen. I'd chanted for a few months, but my practice had petered out until, a couple of years ago, a friend had re-ignited my interest. Chanting helped me to relax and clear my mind but I had remained on the fringes of the Buddhist community, usually chanting with my beads at home in front of a white wall. I had periods of chanting most mornings, then months would pass when I didn't chant at all. I hadn't visited the kaikan all year.

The lunchtime meeting began with twenty minutes of chanting. Afterwards Jimi, who had blue eyes so bright they seemed to emit light like prisms, led a discussion about Buddhism. He was excited about a new book called *The Reluctant Buddhist*.

One of the distinguishing features of Nichiren Buddhism is the belief that earthly desires – beginning with the innate desire to live, breathe, love and procreate – are okay. Unlike more ascetic strands of Buddhism, it does not focus on rising above earthly attachments or your ego. Instead the goal is to purify your desires, so you chant for what will truly bring yourself and others peace and happiness. Compassion, wisdom and courage are the cornerstones to achieve this.

I wanted to know how my son's heart and the experience of carrying a baby with a fatal condition to full term would be interpreted. When the meeting concluded I approached Jimi. 'Is there anyone I might be able to get advice from about a difficult situation?' I asked. Jimi made himself available to talk on the spot. He listened intently, then said, 'In Buddhism we believe we choose our parents and the circumstances of our birth. … The choice reflects whatever karma the baby wishes to transform. So your baby has chosen his heart and chosen you.

'When a person dies, they crystallise the sum of what they have learned during the lifetime. When the opportunity comes to be born again, they take those lessons into the next lifetime.'

'So even if our son has a very short life, it could still serve a purpose?'

'Yes, absolutely. Tremendous value can come from adversity.' I very much liked the idea that our baby could leave having gained something from his brief life and benefited, perhaps, from our care and love for him. I also liked Jimi's conviction that our baby's heart had formed the way it had for a reason. It felt much better than just thinking he and I were victims of a tragic circumstance.

Later that week the real estate agent sent us the builder's and LIM reports for 6 Ariki Road. They revealed some major drawbacks with the property. The foundations needed work, there was borer, and a retaining wall needed rebuilding. Our interest wasn't dampened completely, but we needed to do more research and due diligence.

On Friday morning we revisited the house, this time with a friend who was a builder. It was a clear day and morning sun streamed through the windows in the lounge. The view of sea, sky and hills, with houses, boats and planes in miniature, was as impressive as we remembered.

We looked at the piles under the house. I'd already spoken with a re-piler who thought they could be remedied for under $5,000. I'd also spoken with the author of the builder's report and confirmed the steps we'd need to take to address the borer. A new retaining wall turned out to be non-essential. Our builder friend gave his stamp of approval.

We decided to make an offer on the property the following Monday. My head was in overdrive thinking through the next steps. I compiled a list of people to call – bank, insurance, re-piler. By the afternoon it had all turned to custard. Our bank's insurance company had asked to see the builder's report and said it wouldn't insure the house based on something I hadn't even paid attention to – potential cracks hidden under the recently painted exterior. Not only that, the re-piler had now been persuaded by engineers that all the foundations would need to be redone, at a cost of up to $30,000.

22 weeks

Our baby looked as if he were made from clay. The sonographer had switched on 3D imaging, and instead of glowing luminous white against black shadows as usual, he was now sepia-toned. We could see his features: his nose, the shape of his heel, the swell of his stomach. He had grown a lot and was now too big to see from top to bottom on the screen. We could see only sections of his body.

'Would you mind printing pictures for us?' I asked. I thought Roy could take these to Peru to show his parents.

After the scan, we met Dr D and Louise back in the stuffy meeting room. We hadn't been at this clinic for six weeks, since before our appointment in Auckland and our decision to continue the pregnancy. I wasn't sure if they'd want to keep seeing us since there was no possibility of saving the baby's life, but Dr D said the monthly appointments would continue.

'We'll need to make a plan for the birth,' she said. 'It may be that you have a bit longer with him if we deliver by caesarean, but I'd like to consult my colleagues further about this.'

'How could a caesarean give us more time?' Roy said.

'In a natural delivery there's a possibility his heart could be damaged on exiting the birth canal and that could be the moment he dies.'

'If he is alive at birth, how long might he live for?' I asked.

'I can't honestly tell you.'

'Hours or days?'

'Possibly up to a few days.'

'But won't he die from asphyxiation?' Roy said. This possibility had lodged in his mind after our appointment in Auckland when the doctor had said the baby might not be able to breathe properly.

'No, I don't think baby will die that way. It's more likely to be heart failure,' Dr H said. 'The small pulmonary artery will mean he doesn't get as much oxygen as he should but babies generally deteriorate over days, not moments.'

This was significant news. Our baby's passing might not be quite as immediate as we had thought. I could tell Roy was surprised. He might be able to hold his son and hear him cry. This would give him the tangible, physical experience I was already having as the baby prodded, kicked and thumped inside me. A thought crossed my mind: if our son lived for days, instead of minutes or hours, would the goodbye be even more painful?

'Do you think I should begin readying myself to say goodbye to my baby now?'

'I think you need to stay in the present with your baby, respond to the reality at hand. If you begin to let him go now you might miss out on bonding with him and the experience of loving him fully,' Camilla said.

After I'd spoken to Jimi at the kaikan, he had orchestrated a meeting with Camilla, another Buddhist who might be able to offer support. Camilla had her own story of miscarriage and a long road to conceiving a healthy child. In the kaikan's small chanting room, we sat on the floor on large navy-blue cushions with white origami shapes.

'I want to do my very best for my baby and give him all the love I can.'

'Your baby will also want to do his best by you and love you. As much as you're his protector, he is yours. He's your bodhisattva. A bodhisattva is an agent for enlightenment, someone who is dedicated to the happiness of others. Buddhism says all children are their parents' teachers; they have evolved further than us.' Camilla's eyebrows rose in enthusiasm as she spoke and her sentences often ended in exclamation marks.

I was surprised. I'd been thinking the responsibility was all mine, as the mother, to protect my baby. I remembered Father Lyons' story about St Christopher and the baby who guided him to the other side of the river. It contained a similar message.

Camilla went on to tell me about a woman she'd met who had a remarkable presence and grace. 'I found out later her first baby had died in her arms on a flight back to see her family in the UK. While this was a terrible thing to have happened, somehow the experience had turned her into an incredible person.

'You might have made a contract with your baby to have this experience with him. Maybe ultimately it will be for the good of both of you.'

This was a challenging thought, but there was empowerment in it too. As I'd felt after speaking with Jimi, it was refreshing not to be cast as a tragic victim.

That weekend, Camilla invited women who practised Nichiren Buddhism in Wellington to come and chant for me and my baby, and also for a four-month-old baby with a rare and potentially fatal condition. On Saturday morning, before I'd even walked through the doors of the kaikan, I could hear the hum of voices. They sounded like honey bees buzzing around a garden in summer. For a moment I was overwhelmed. I bit my lip to stop tears from falling. Camilla saw me and held my hand as we entered the room full of chanting women. She had mobilised a small Buddhist army.

On either side of the altar with its gohonzon, a venerated religious scroll, there were posters saying: 'Please chant for Emma and baby, and Maki and baby Julian.' At first I could only sit with the chanting beads in my hands and tears rolling down my face. In that moment I felt the full weight of the situation I was in and grief at the thought of my darling boy's condition, yet I also felt great compassion around me, a universal desire to protect mothers and our young. I began to chant, and bit by bit I felt stronger and more peaceful.

After the chanting I was presented with my own gohonzon, membership of SGI, the Soka Gakkai International Buddhist Association, and the loan of a wooden altar. I felt touched that people I didn't know had been willing to chant for my baby and me, and filled with gratitude.

Paula, the real estate agent, got in touch with a new proposal from the owner of 6 Ariki Road. The owner would commission the work to be done on the foundations; we could make an offer subject to the work being completed. In the meantime, the house had been taken off the market. Paula explained the owner was in hospital, having had a heart attack.

I wasn't sure. The issues with the house had given me cold feet. I decided to tour some more open homes to remind myself what was out there. Four open homes later I had been convinced that few homes in our price range had the wow factor of 6 Ariki Road and almost all needed work of some kind. We spoke with a mortgage broker, who advised us not to put in an offer yet. However, we still had a problem: where would we live when we moved out of our current rental?

'Maybe we could offer to rent Ariki Road in the interim,' Roy suggested. I doubted the owner would agree, but we could ask.

23 weeks

'Have you checked to make sure the cardboard packing boxes in the garage haven't got damp?' I asked Roy. 'What about those two old bikes in the garage – what are you going to do with them?'

I'd been dropping hints for a few days that Roy should start packing. While he was away I'd be moving house or putting all our belongings into storage – we still didn't know which. The owner of 6 Ariki Road was considering our rental proposal but nothing had been confirmed. What we did know was that we had to vacate our house next month when Roy would be in Peru. I wanted him to pack up his things before he left.

The week of his departure had snuck up on us. Roy had been burning the midnight oil, working like a man possessed on the academic paper he was presenting at a conference for Bayesian statisticians in Cancún. He was leaving Wellington on Tuesday for a two-day conference in Auckland before flying out to Mexico on Friday. On Wednesday, I was going to fly to Auckland to farewell him and see my family.

Despite my hints, by the morning of Roy's departure from Wellington he still hadn't packed a single thing, never mind the luggage for his trip. I left for work gritting my teeth and telling myself to trust him. He would do things in his own way.

My softly-softly approach dissolved that evening when I arrived home to a cold dark house. It was six o'clock and I was due to take Roy to the airport at six-thirty. I walked from room to room, noting with dismay the lopsided pyramids of books and papers still stacked on his desk, his cluttered bedside table, his football knick-knacks on the shelves, the washing basket overflowing with his dirty clothes.

And then I got mad. Really mad. I was the one who would have to shoulder the responsibility of packing and moving the bulk of our household when six months pregnant, while he was away globetrotting.

Roy arrived home minutes later.

'Why haven't you packed?'

'What do you mean I haven't packed?' He was genuinely surprised. 'My wardrobe is cleared, I've got rid of the bikes and taken boxes of books to store at uni.'

Furiously, I listed all the things he hadn't done. In response, like a whirling dervish, he scooped the contents of his desk into boxes, tipped his dirty washing into large plastic bags, taped up boxes, chucked things in the bin. By six-forty we still hadn't left the house. It would be his problem if he missed his plane, I fumed.

We arrived at the airport in the nick of time. As I left the airport carpark my phone beeped with a text – 'Thanks Emsy, you are awesome and I'm missing you already.' I smiled. I hoped I'd be able to farewell him in Auckland on Friday in a more relaxed style.

In Auckland Roy had bought a vast collection of goods to take to his family in Peru, including a breadmaker and countless groceries. At the airport we looked like one of those huddles of people I'd pitied in the past, belongings spilling out on to the floor as bags are repacked. When a large red and blue striped plastic bag Roy had bought to carry the excess luggage was ready to be closed, the zip broke. Luckily he had also brought a roll of masking tape, which he now wound round and round the bag.

'Is the masking tape going to hold? Why don't we use this bag instead?' Roy had bought two bags and I opened the second one.

'What are you doing?' he snapped.

'Trying to help you, as I've been trying to do all day,' I snapped back.

At last the bags were packed, sealed and checked in. It was time to say goodbye. I tried to swallow down my irritation, to make this a good moment between us. I had a gift for Roy: a St Christopher's medallion like the one Father Lyons had given me. I had also taken a selfie of my pregnant figure and printed it and some other photos to make a little album.

Roy lifted my top and kissed my stomach.

'I love you Jesús Valentino and I love you, Emsy,' he said.

I softened. Despite our tense moments, I had been feeling very much in love with Roy. His story was knitted into mine in a way I'd never experienced before with a partner. It was a shock on Sunday night to arrive back home to a cold silent house.

24 weeks

Vicki was talking about a new prototype 'cuddle cot' for deceased babies. It had a cooling system, so the body of a baby laid on it wouldn't deteriorate as fast as normal. 'If you like,' she said, 'you could be the first family to try it out.'

We were sitting in my lounge, talking over tea. Vicki had offered to visit and had bought along Joan Curle, an English woman who was also involved in Sands. While both Joan and Vicki had lost babies, enough time had passed that they seemed able to talk easily, even enthusiastically, about what to do after a baby died.

'Although they try to get it right, hospital staff are sometimes unsure about how to support grieving parents,' Joan said. 'Midwives have jobs to do, like taking weights and measurements. If you don't want that to happen at the time, it's okay to say, 'No, I just want to hold my baby.' As parents you are the ones in control.' She described being present at the birth of a relative's twenty-week-old baby girl, who had a condition where amniotic fluid continually seeps through the skin. She helped to dress and re-dress the deceased baby when her clothes became wet.

Sands' philosophy was to encourage families to make memories with their deceased babies. You could take handprints and footprints, even have a baby's foot cast in bronze. The organisation supplied Wellington Hospital with woven Moses baskets for babies to be carried in. The baskets came filled with memory books, toys, clothes for tiny babies who had been born prematurely, and knitted angels.

'I think losing a baby is life-changing,' Joan said. 'For me it was a more profound grief than losing a parent or sibling.' That was a scary thought.

Vicki and Joan, generous caring women, were trying to equip me with information and ideas to make the forecasted birth and death of our son as positive an experience as it could be, or perhaps the least negative. But I wasn't at ease with the conversation. It was difficult to think about these things. It felt premature to begin planning the practicalities of the farewell when my baby boy was still so very alive inside me. I was still getting to know him. How could I do that properly if I was already saying goodbye?

Our conversation was interrupted when Vicki received a call from a distraught Sands member. She was at a playground on the nearby waterfront, where a baby had been found buried under a pōhutukawa tree. A note had been left telling the baby it was loved. It was signed by the parents and grandparents. It was unclear what the circumstances were. The police had arrived. They would have to dig up the tiny body and treat the place as a crime scene. The situation was deeply upsetting. I felt winded just hearing about it. I wondered what had made the family want to bury the remains where they had. In Māori culture the roots of the pōhutukawa tree are thought to lead to the underworld, so perhaps that was why they had chosen it. I hoped the bodily remains would be treated with tenderness and care.

'We can't really get involved, not unless the family can be identified and wants our support,' Vicki sighed.

After Vicki and Joan left I saw I'd received a text from my friend Olivia. The last time I'd seen Olivia, several weeks before, she'd thought she might be pregnant. She was planning to take a test on her partner's birthday. I had wondered if I would feel unconditionally happy for her if the test was positive and she went on to have a healthy baby. Or would I ask myself why her and not me?

The text said she'd been planning to call me to tell me she was indeed pregnant, but had miscarried overnight. I felt the aching heaviness in her few simple sentences. Later that week my friend Clarinda called. She had decided on a termination, doubting she had any real future with James, the father of the child, and not wishing to become a solo mother.

After the termination she and James had slept together again once or twice. A condom had failed so she'd taken a morning-after pill. A few weeks later, when her period hadn't arrived, she'd taken a pregnancy test. It was positive. When she went into a clinic to have this confirmed, the staff found the egg was actually unfertilised, a 'blighted ovum'.

She was booked in for dilation and curettage, a procedure to clean her out her uterus, a week later. When she went in for this procedure, the doctors found a baby's heartbeat. Against all odds, Clarinda was pregnant again. She must have conceived a mere two weeks after her termination. This time she felt she couldn't farewell another baby. 'But I don't think James is the man for me and I'm terrified by the idea of bringing up a child alone. This is not how I imagined bringing a child into the world,' she told me.

It was astonishing to be hearing all these stories in one week. Stories of babies who were wanted but lost, and babies who weren't wanted but came into being anyway. These realities co-exist. In the end, for all we may wish to control the conception of a baby we can't. We are at the mercy of forces we may not always understand.

Since Joan and Vicki's visit I'd wanted to push away their words, but questions swirled in my head. Was I right to let myself blithely enjoy a baby who was alive and well in the present, without thinking too much about the future? Or would it be wiser to begin preparing myself to farewell him?

In her memoir *The Long Goodbye* about her mother's death, Meghan O'Rourke writes about anticipatory grief – the intense grieving you can experience while waiting for a loved one to die. 'I thought of my anticipation a lot,' she says, 'picturing it as an invader come to rob me of my joy, a stealthy, quilled creature of the night, a fear that wouldn't let me sit still.' I wasn't ready to welcome in that stealthy, quilled creature of the night. I didn't think I'd be a good mother if I did.

On the other hand, I didn't want to be in a state of denial. As much as I loved our baby, I had to accept he was going to pass quickly through this world. I didn't want to pretend there was an easy road ahead for us.

If Roy had been there, I would have discussed these ideas with him. He would have sat next to me on the sofa and held my hand while Vicki and Joan discussed dressing dead babies. I realised that having him at my side had been a big part of what'd made me feel I was strong enough for the journey. In the last week I'd rattled around our home, uncomfortable in the silence, unaccustomed to making solitary decisions. Since Roy's departure we'd barely communicated. There had been mixed-up time zones, bad internet connections, and Roy's busy conference agenda.

25 weeks

Our landlord knew I was pregnant, but I hadn't told him about our baby's condition. Now he'd sent me an email saying his wife was just finishing a spring-cleaning of their youngest baby's toys:

> Our children were the first grandchildren our parents had and they inundated us with toys, many of which have barely been played with. Would you like them? I appreciate that now might not be the best time to be taking on more things, as you will be moving soon, so no worries if you don't want the added hassle. But happy to bring them by if you think they will be useful for the little one.

How to respond? The landlord was rather reserved. I felt it would be uncomfortable explaining our baby's condition to him, and he would probably feel uncomfortable hearing about it. I was becoming choosy about who I talked to. I veered away from incidental conversations about my pregnancy with strangers at the supermarket, or on the bus. I was trying to protect myself from reactions of shock and pity. There is power in the thoughts and feelings that others project upon you. If I were over-exposed I might come to believe that the people who saw us as a tragedy were right.

After deliberating I decided to accept the toys. I figured that some would be nice to have for our baby and I could give the rest to my stepbrother's girlfriend, Jaimie, who was now eight months pregnant and having her baby shower the following weekend. 'Everyone will understand if you don't want to come,' my father had said. It was another strange decision to have to make. On the one hand I didn't want to appear churlish. I wasn't jealous that Jaimie's baby was healthy and mine wasn't.

What felt hard was the thought of lots of women talking excitedly about newborns, offering advice on teething and colic, remembering sleepless nights and bestowing their blessings. The different future facing my baby and me would be bought into sharp relief. I was wary of entertaining comparisons that could slide me into self-pity. I needed to stay strong and accept the cards we'd been dealt.

In the end I decided not to go but I bought Jaimie some bath toys and two tiny checked shirts for her baby. I delivered these on the evening after her shower. Their house was still filled with leftover macaroons and cream cake and biscuits. She had been given a beautiful wooden bassinet by a friend of a family for whom I used to nanny. Perhaps the bassinet would have been offered it to me under other circumstances. I directed my mind away from the thought.

'Yesterday I caught the bus to Tulum. Did you know they have Mayan ruins right on the sea cliffs? Oh my god, the water was so warm. I found out there were sharks *after* I went swimming.' Roy grinned. We finally had a working Skype connection after a week of failed attempts. 'I forgot what good value Mexican restaurants are. Even when you order a beer you get a little plate of snacks.'

Roy was wearing a singlet and his skin was burnished a deep tan. He continued to regale me with stories about the tacos he'd eaten, the heat, the interesting conference sessions. I waited for him to ask me how I was faring at home alone in the depths of winter, trying to sort out where we were going to live.

'Sorry, Emsy, I've got to go. The next conference session is about to start,' Roy said.

'But we haven't talked about Ariki Road.'

'I'll try calling you later.'

I was nonplussed as the call ended. Along with my desire for a little sympathy, we needed to talk for practical reasons. The owner of 6 Ariki Road had agreed to let us rent the house while work was carried out on the foundations. The re-piler had confirmed we could live in the house while new concrete piles were being installed. This was good news, but if we were going to move in I wanted to be pretty certain we would eventually buy the house – otherwise we'd have to move out again in a few months when the owner wanted it back on the property market.

I'd been researching whether the house's brick and mortar structure was likely to cause problems in the future. Earthquake-strengthening houses cost a bomb. At the city council a housing inspector had offered to come and take a look. 'I don't think retro-earthquake-strengthening regulations for residential homes will change in my lifetime,' he said. He emailed me his assessment of the house, including maintenance work he thought it would need.

This had put my mind at ease. I was feeling surer that buying 6 Ariki Rd was a good idea. In the meantime, renting it and moving in would mean we could 'try before we buy', a luxury in the game of house-purchasing. But I still needed to talk this through with Roy.

He called later that afternoon when I was on my way to my first pre-natal yoga class. 'Tell me what you want from me,' he said regarding Ariki Road.

'I don't want anything,' I said. 'We're thinking about buying this house and we need to do it together. Did you read the email from the council engineer?'

'No, I haven't had the chance.'

'I also spoke to the re-piler, who said we could live in the house while the work is done on the foundations.'

'Okay.'

'Roy, this is important. Could you make more of an effort.'

'You're stressing about nothing. What am I supposed to do from here anyway?'

The phone call was cut short as I was running late. At the yoga class, I bit my lip to stem my tears as we did the first breathing exercises. The dissonance of the day's conversations with Roy clanged inside me.

'If you had a caesarean, you would be numb from the waist down for three hours afterwards. Immediately after delivery your stomach would need to be stitched up.'

I was having my monthly check-up and Tessa and I were picking up on the conversation from the last appointment with the maternal foetal medicine team, where Dr D had said I might have longer with my baby if he were delivered by caesarean.

'So, if I had a caesarean I wouldn't be able to take my baby immediately into my arms?'

'No.'

I imagined myself lying on the table with a drip in one arm and a pulse monitor in the other, wanting to hold my baby, not knowing how long he would live. Being able to move freely seemed important. If I had a caesarean I would also need to spend extra time in hospital afterwards, the recovery time would be longer than for a natural birth, my fertility would be slightly reduced, and the operation might affect how I gave birth in the future.

On the other hand, our son's heart could be damaged exiting the birth canal. It could twist on its veins. It could get stuck. That could be the moment he died. Neither caesarean or natural birth were straightforward options.

26 weeks

'We have to decide once and for all about Ariki Road.'

As I spoke Roy looked at me with glazed, distant eyes. It was six p.m. in New Zealand and one a.m. in Peru. For the next four weeks he would be staying with his parents in Lima. My sympathy with his fatigue was limited. It was crunch time. In three weeks I had to move out of our house.

'I don't know, Emma. The email from the council guy has given me some doubts. "Regular and ongoing maintenance would be required to ensure the security of the dwelling."'

'Yes, his assessment said the house needs maintenance, but we already knew that. The important thing he said was that we wouldn't be facing an earthquake-strengthening bill any time soon.'

'Well, the owner is being too greedy about the rental price anyway. We shouldn't pay $430 when there will be disruptions with the foundation work.'

'Let's make a counter offer. What do you think? $400?'

'Why don't you just move in with Amy?'

'No, I want to be permanently settled somewhere.'

'Just because you don't want to move twice,' he said.

'Oh, so I'm being lazy because I don't want to be looking for a house when I'm eight months pregnant and about to give birth to a baby with a fatal heart condition?'

I felt as though Roy was pulling the rug from under my feet. He hadn't been paying attention to the developments I'd been emailing him and now he wanted to use his power of veto.

'Roy, you've left me alone to manage a house move. I've been doing all the donkey work while you're off having a good time in Mexico. Can't you see we need a home?'

Lightning fast, I felt the sum of everything I resented in our relationship. I did the lion's share of the cooking and cleaning, organised all the logistics, did the driving, paid the phone bills. 'You are so selfish,' I said. 'I'd be better off just finding a house for me and our baby by myself. I can't count on you for anything.'

Seconds later I hung up. It was probably for the best: I was scared by what violent thing I might say to Roy next. I forced myself to make a cup of tea. I told myself that laying blame was not going to help anything, although 'ROY, IT'S YOUR FAULT' was written like a glaring neon sign in my head.

Ten minutes later, I called him back.

'Okay. Let's move into Ariki Road. But we need to ask to pay less rent,' he said.

'Yes, sure, we can do that.'

I tried to move on to lighter topics of conversation, but Roy was now remote and wary. I could tell his heart wasn't in it. Afterwards I wondered what damage I'd done. Roy wasn't going to be missing me from the other side of the world, and being so far away we couldn't forgive each other over dinner or in bed. I imagined him meeting a trim Latina statistician, who would look at him with big pretty eyes and engage him in conversation. Affairs happened at conferences all the time, didn't they? I knew this was a silly paranoid thought and yet I allowed myself to get on board with it.

'Your baby's heart rate is slower than normal, 100 beats per minute,' Dr D said. I'd had the usual scan and we were now in the meeting room.

'What should his heart rate be?'

'The normal range is 130 to 160. When a baby's heart rates slow to 55 we start getting really worried.'

It could be the node that controls heart rate hadn't formed properly, she said. It could be natural variance. They didn't propose to do anything. In an otherwise healthy baby, a slow heart rate might lead to a recommendation of an early caesarean.

The news was a small jolt: our baby might not make it to full term. Stillbirth was a possibility. I hadn't really countenanced this. Despite his heart, the baby had continued to grow well, all his measurements in the scans were well above average, and he was wriggly and active.

'Have you thought about birth options?' Dr D said.

'I'm keen to hear your recommendation. You said last time you wanted to consult your colleagues.'

'We'd recommend a natural birth. We don't know if a caesarean would give you any more time with your baby, but a natural birth would be better for your health.'

'And what if his heart is damaged in the birth canal, or if it's bleeding when he's born?'

'Actually, I've asked a neonatologist to come and talk about his care after he's born.'

Shortly afterwards Dr W arrived. He was English, although he could have passed for Swedish with his pale skin and light blonde hair. His gaze was direct, and he had an air of efficiency.

'If your baby's heart is bleeding at birth we'll swaddle it with gauze. There's nothing we can do to treat it,' he said.

'And what if he has problems breathing? Would you give him oxygen?'

'If he's not breathing we'll make him comfortable with morphine. We won't put him on a respirator. Babies don't like tubes up their noses. Our aim is to make it possible for you to give him lots of cuddles. He doesn't need interventions, he needs to be with you.'

I didn't disagree with Dr W's sentiment. If our baby had just a short while to live, quality time with him would be the most important thing. But she was so black and white in how she said this, as if there was no room for negotiation, no other options for palliative care, when previously it had been hinted there might be. There was no more talk, either, of having a cardiologist on hand when he was born. It was a lot to process. Afterwards, more than anything I needed to talk to Roy.

'They're not willing to do anything to prolong his life. They just want to cover his heart with gauze and give him morphine. And his heart rate is slower than it should be,' I told Roy on Skype that evening.

Roy was particularly concerned about the heart rate. He had not said so directly but I knew he was worried our baby would die while he was away.

'Emsy, we've just got to have faith in our son. There's nothing else we can do. We've got to hope and pray that everything will turn out okay.'

We talked for three hours. Roy had been making wholemeal bread for his family in the breadmaker. Peruvians are accustomed to white bread and he'd received an offer from the local health food shop to buy his bread. I sang the praises of my new wool-lined slippers. I told him how our son's kicks and punches were getting more vigorous and were a pleasant, secret distraction during work meetings. We'd settled on a rental price with the owner of 6 Ariki Road of $400 per week, with an extra reduction when the re-piling was under way. Each little piece of news bridged the gap between us.

'I love you, Emsy, and I love you, hijito Jesús Valentino,' he said as we ended the call. Roy had continued to call our son Jesús Valentino and through dint of repetition the name didn't sound as outlandish as I'd first thought. Maybe our son with his extraordinary heart deserved an extraordinary name.

27 weeks

Baby Julian's face was as round as a beach ball. Rolls of fat made his five-month-old legs a landscape of hills and valleys. I was struck by his peaceful air. He was like a Buddha baby, surrounded by offerings of tinkling rattles, rainbow-coloured soft toys and gently turning mobiles. It was hard to believe his life was hanging in the balance. His rare condition meant he couldn't produce the enzymes to digest fats, and exposure to them could produce a potentially fatal reaction in his muscles and heart. If he reached the age of two the doctors thought he would be likely to survive, but they couldn't give any guarantees.

I was visiting Julian and his mother Maki with my Buddhist friends Jimi and Camilla. We sat on the floor in the lounge in front of Maki's gohonzon altar and chanted for Julian's health. As we chanted, the baby looked on bemusedly.

Given the severity of Maki's situation, Jimi had brought her a small gift from SGI President Ikeda, imbued with his desire to impart deep encouragement to her.

Chanting's promise to induce a positive state of mind did seem to be delivering results. I was feeling uncharacteristically calm about the next fortnight's two big deadlines. The first was to finish writing my organisation's annual report, my major work project of the year. The second was to move out of our house.

Moving house generally takes me to the brink of my stress levels but I was determined to stay on an even keel. I'd already begun sorting and discarding, sifting through my dozens of scarves, throwing out half the contents of bathroom cupboards. I'd been inundated with offers to help, including from Roy's three best friends in Wellington, Javier, Nacho and Josue. I had booked house movers with a truck for the following weekend, but I would ask these friends to help move breakable items by car. My mother and my sister Phoebe were also flying down to help. All in all, the pending move was feeling surprisingly under control.

I'd already begun decorating the Ariki Road house in my head – placing paintings on the walls, thinking about colour schemes. I'd been buying things too, quite a lot of things in fact: a retro mustard-coloured sofa, red patterned cushions, an Indian tablecloth, aquamarine bedside tables, saucepans, a frying pan, a knife, new photo frames. I was eyeing up coffee tables. I suddenly had a manic interest in home decorating. I imagined this was a result of pregnancy hormones and the nesting instinct kicking in.

28 weeks

Despite my calm of the week before, I was awake at five-thirty on Tuesday morning thinking about the annual report. My deadline for the first draft was the close of business next day. I'd found anomalies in some of the data. I needed to raise these with the business analyst and confirm the correct figures.

That day and the next, adrenaline kicked in. I edited the financial statements, wrote about the year's communications activities, penned the reports of the chief executive and chairperson. By six on Wednesday evening I'd emailed the thirty-page draft to the CEO and senior management for feedback. There would be more work to do next week to incorporate this feedback and liaise with designers.

That night a set of keys for Ariki Road was dropped off by a friend of the owner. My attention switched to the week's next challenge: Saturday's house move. On Thursday I cleaned boxes that had been sitting in the garage and stacked them in the hallway, bought tape for sealing them, asked at the local shop for newspapers, and began packing up kitchen cupboards. I ventured into the garage and opened the door of my 1985 Mercedes, our second car, which had sat neglected for months. Luckily it still started. I drove it to the petrol station carwash and vacuumed it. I needed to sell the car and at least now it was reasonably clean.

By then it was late afternoon. My back was aching and I was hobbling. Was this due to the weight of my belly? The stretching of ligaments? I'd had a dream run with the pregnancy so far, with no difficult symptoms, but maybe my luck was about to turn.

All Friday my mother and sister worked like mad, packing up the kitchen, bedrooms and laundry. Late in the afternoon we went to the new house, where we opened windows and cleaned the floors. At five o'clock Roy's friends arrived with the breakables. I opened one of Roy's bottles of Peruvian Pisco. We stood in the lounge and toasted the new house. From the enormous windows the Remutaka hills could be seen turning mauve in the setting sun.

On Saturday the movers arrived an hour late, knackered from a job they'd done that morning. When they parked the truck I saw the look of fear as they took in the steep flight of ninety-five steps up to the house. For more than an hour they sweated and heaved. At the end they looked like wilted plants but everything was unloaded.

Meanwhile, though, I'd discovered there was no hot water in the house. I texted the owner, who gave me the number of an electrician. He said he would send someone on Monday.

By the end of the next day I was so tired with unpacking I could barely think straight. It was a freezing winter's night and I discovered that, even with a fire blazing in the lounge, 6 Ariki Road was a cold, cold house. It was so cold I wore a hat in the kitchen while I heated a packet of soup for my sister Phoebe, who was staying on, and me. I would have liked nothing more than to curl up in front of the telly, only we couldn't get the telly working.

29 weeks

That week I had an appointment with Tessa. These would be fortnightly now I was in the third trimester. Tessa listened to my baby's heartbeat with the Doppler ultrasound pressed up to my belly. It was still slow, ninety-five beats per minute. 'The fact his heart rate increases when he moves is a good sign and he's still growing,' Tessa said, to reassure me.

I asked her whether she thought I should again raise the possibility of giving our baby oxygen if he needed it at birth when we met the specialist next. The ruling from Dr W that nothing would be done to help our son live even a little longer still rankled. All birthing units were equipped with oxygen masks for babies. I didn't understand why this wouldn't be an option for our baby.

'I can understand their point of view,' Tessa said. 'If you start giving a baby oxygen, where do you stop?'

'The possibilities in the universe are limitless and so too are the possibilities for your baby. These extend across lifetimes.' Jimi's perspective was almost exactly opposite to that of the hospital staff.

He, Camilla and SGI Buddhists Anne, Miki, Nedra and Amber had braved the pelting rain and howling wind to trek up to my house and chant with me. I was amazed by these kind Buddhists and their dedication to supporting me and my baby. In the past I'd been fiercely independent, believing I needed to solve my problems in private.

The equation was different now. It wasn't only my wellbeing at stake but the life of my baby, and I was open to anything I thought might benefit him.

'I feel my baby is lucky to be receiving so much love and I believe it will be put to good use, even if I don't know how. I feel so grateful for all the compassion I've received. It makes me want to be a more compassionate person myself,' I said.

That week, too, I saw Father Lyons, who quietly baptised our baby in the womb in case he didn't make it to full term. Something had been playing on my mind. I realised Father Lyons assumed I was Catholic and I hadn't found the right moment to correct him. I had nervously written an email saying that, while I believed in God, I wasn't raised with any religion and also believed in Buddhist teachings. His response had surprised me with its kindness:

Emma – lovely to get your message and thank you for explaining your situation. You are very welcome here. The most important thing to me is people's sincerity, and your evident love for Roy and your child and the depth of your faith which tells me of your love also for God, are more than enough to accept and bless you. Anytime you wish to chat I will make myself available. Wishing you the deep peace that comes with the presence of God.

Father Lyons was challenging my stereotypes about fire-and-brimstone preachers, and guilt being a hallmark of the Catholic faith.

As I thought about my baby's heart growing outside his chest, I kept being drawn to images of the sacred heart. Worship of this dates back to seventeenth-century France, when St Marguerite-Marie Alacoque had visions of Christ showing her his heart, which was brighter than the sun and gave off flames. The crown of thorns that often encircles images of the sacred heart represents the wounds suffered by Jesus, while the rays of light around it suggest the transformative power of divine love.

30 weeks

I didn't know whether Roy would be driving me to the hospital when the moment came, or we'd be calling a cab and hoping the driver could handle the moans of a labouring woman in the back seat. It all depended on whether Roy got a driver's licence. His latest plan was to apply for one in Peru, where licences were issued on the spot to people who passed the practical driving test.

Under the system, hopefuls assembled at a stadium, where they had to navigate a driving route and a series of obstacles while being observed by examiners from a watchtower. Roy had already failed this test once. After he made an error, an examiner had instructed him via a loudspeaker to exit the circuit.

He'd had no better luck trying to get his licence in New Zealand: he'd sat the road code test twice and flunked both times. Since the beginning of the year I'd got him the road code booklet from the library, offered to help him study it, and periodically given him lectures in the hope of jolting him out of procrastination, all to no avail. Now I found myself getting furious as I imagined him coming home still with no licence. I sent him a none too subtle email: 'How are the driving lessons going? Please remember your son and I are counting on you.'

The subject line read: 'Guess who got their licence?' Attached was a photo of a Peruvian driving licence with Roy's photo on it. Ten minutes later the phone rang.

'I did it!'

'That's awesome. Well done.'

'My hand hurts a bit though.'

After being issued his licence, in his elation Roy had punched a wall. I realised getting his licence had meant as much to him as it did to me. And he was going to be home in just over a week.

31 weeks

'Roy a salido de Santiago y estará en Nueva Zelanda en ocho horas. ¿Me entiendes?'

Señor Valerio's voice was insistent.

Roy… left Santiago … eight hours … New Zealand … understand? It was 12.45 a.m. I didn't quite understand why Roy's father had called. Had Roy's flight been delayed? Had something gone wrong?

'Si, voy al aeropuerto por Roycito en la mañana. ¿Si? ¿Nada a cambiado?'

'Así es, Emma. Un abrazo y adiós.'

I lay awake, fretting I hadn't fully grasped the message. The past week I'd been counting down the days to Roy's arrival. I couldn't wait to wrap my arms around him. I'd been doing some final decorating at Ariki Road. I'd hung pictures and tidied the spare room-cum-office. I'd bought Roy a large desk, and filled the fridge with nice food. An uncle who came to stay had set about trimming trees that blocked light from some windows. I wanted everything to be just right so Roy would walk in and love the place.

At the airport, tears welled in my eyes as he emerged from the sky tunnel. His energy fizzed about me. He kissed the tears on my cheeks. 'I can't get my arms around you anymore,' he joked as he hugged me.

Back home he opened his suitcases and drew out presents. There were baby clothes from his mother; a fine alpaca scarf for me; a couple of riotously coloured ponchos, one for an adult and one for a baby.

'Jesús Valentino, do you like the poncho? Do you want to be in the danza de la pluma?' Roy addressed my stomach.

I'd decided to stop putting up a fight against the name Roy wanted for our son. Who cared how it sounded to the rest of the world.

A few days earlier I'd booked a holiday to Tonga, throwing caution to the wind and following my instincts that despite my advanced stage of pregnancy everything would be okay. My friends Amy and Mandy were coming with me to swim with whales. I was leaving in two weeks.

Roy couldn't exactly tell me not to go, having just come back from jet-setting himself, but he was worried about my safety.

'What if you go into labour over there?'

'Well, it's only a three-hour flight from New Zealand and Mum's babies were all born after their due date.'

That afternoon, keen to show off his new skills, he proudly drove me around our suburb at twenty kilometres an hour.

Afterwards we picked up Indian takeaways. Back home we lit a fire, curled up on the couch, and watched a Bruce Lee movie on TV.

Prompted perhaps by the martial arts yells or the heat of the curry, the baby kicked wildly.

'Jesús Valentino,' Roy said, 'do you want to be like Bruce Lee?'

32 weeks

¿Cómo estás, Jesús Valentino? ¿Cómo estás?

¡Muy bien!

Este es un saludo de amistad

¡Qué bien!

Haremos lo posible por hacer muchos amigos

¿Cómo estás, Jesús Valentino? ¿Cómo estás?

¡Muy bien!

In the mornings Roy had taken to diving under the duvet and singing to his son. 'How are you, Jesús Valentino? How are you? Very well! This is a greeting of friendship. That's great! We'll do what we can to make lots of friends. How are you, Jesús Valentino? How are you? Very well!' The song had the same tune as 'If you're happy and you know it, clap your hands'.

He continued the tête-à-tête with his son, whose name we'd begun shortening to JV. 'Buenos días, hijito. ¿Cómo estás, JV? ¿Bien? Hoy día tenemos sol y voy a hacer huevos para tu desayuno.' 'Good morning, little son. How are you, JV? Well? Today we have sun and I'm going to make eggs for your breakfast.'

I was glad to see Roy enjoying being a father-to-be. It was so good to have him back. He made coffee in the morning, stocked up the wood supply and introduced me to our next-door neighbours. His arrival coincided with the first week of spring. The bitterly cold days of August were replaced by milder weather and the scent of spring flowers.

I felt happy. Maybe it was my rising levels of oxytocin, the hormone of love. Maybe it was the awareness of the preciousness of this time with our baby. When I rested my hand on my stomach and felt a heel or knee I thought of Pablo Neruda's sonnet about the plant that carries inwardly the light of hidden flowers.

'Your baby's growth is above average, but his heart rate is still slow,' Dr D said. We were at our next maternal foetal medicine appointment.

'Given his heart is so fragile, don't you think it would be better for Emma to have a caesarean?' Roy said.

'We don't really know if a caesarean would mean a better outcome for your baby, but there are advantages for Emma and future pregnancies in having a natural birth,' Dr D replied.

Roy hadn't been here for the last discussions about this. I'd filled him in via Skype, but the implications were only now dawning on him.

'And if he's not breathing when he's born?'

'Dr W, the neonatologist, doesn't recommend any interventions. If your baby is on a respirator machine in an incubator you may have less quality time with him. There's a risk he will die there, instead of in your arms.'

'Couldn't he be given oxygen via a mask if he needs it, though?' I asked. 'If it would give us even another half an hour with our baby I think it would be worth it.'

'We could ask Dr W. I'll invite him to your next appointment so he can talk things through with Roy too. If the plan isn't clear to everyone, one of the more aggressive neonatologists might attempt to do more.' It wasn't clear to me what attempting to do more might involve, or what the other options were.

'It's like they're just giving up on him,' Roy said as we sat having coffee in a nearby café.

'I know what you mean. I do want him in our arms, but I don't understand why they wouldn't give him an oxygen mask.'

Afterwards we went for a stroll in the Botanic Garden. I found a bench with a view over the city. 'No, let's sit here instead,' Roy said, pointing to another bench. As we got closer we saw it had a bronze plaque attached: 'James Edwards, born to eternal life, 30.08.12.' A baby who had died. It was pure coincidence that we'd chosen to sit there but I was hardly surprised.

On Saturday morning over breakfast I played Roy Chris Knox's beautiful love song 'Not Given Lightly'. Roy, in turn, played Israel Kamakawiwo'ole's version of 'Somewhere Over The Rainbow'.

'I wonder if that would be a good song to play at JV's funeral?' I said.

I wasn't sure whether I should say this thought out loud. When I'd tried to broach the subject of what we wanted to happen after the baby died, Roy had shut down the conversation, saying, 'Let's just face the things we need to face when we need to face them.'

Now he broke into sobs. 'I was thinking that the next time we see JV will be somewhere over the rainbow,' he said.

I sat on Roy's knee and held his head to my chest, stroking his hair, searching for words of comfort, the things I'd been telling myself. 'Remember our baby doesn't want to bring us sadness. Our job is to love him whatever happens, even if that means letting him go.'

33 weeks

Twenty-six pairs of eyes watched intently as the plastic head of a baby doll was manoeuvred through a model pelvis. It was a tight squeeze. The doll didn't look as though it'd make it.

'Right at the end, baby needs to twist its shoulders to get itself through,' Kass the midwife was saying. But how would a baby know to do this? It was like expecting someone to do a tricky parallel parking move when they'd never reversed before. It looked as feasible as passing a motion the size of a rock melon or sneezing a whole strawberry out of your nose. Yet apparently all this could happen easily and instinctively if the labour was going well.

We were sitting in a circle of chairs in a community hall with thirteen other couples. I'd hesitated about signing up to the antenatal class, unsure how I'd feel in a room full of pregnant couples with very different expectations. Yet I still needed to know how to give birth. When Tessa had asked me to think about writing a birth plan, it had felt like being asked to write a plan for landing on the moon, so little did I know.

We'd decided to attend just the first two of eight classes, the ones that covered birth. The class had begun with a round of introductions. I hadn't wanted to reveal our son's condition, imagining the dropped jaws and silence of a group of people we didn't know. Luckily the brief was restricted to saying how many weeks pregnant we were, where we would give birth, if this was our first birth experience, who our midwife was, and what we expected to get out of the classes.

Now Kass was saying, 'Your labour might begin with a "show", where the mucous plug that has been stopping up the cervix comes out. It looks like a few tablespoons of bloody phlegm. It sometimes gives women the fright of their lives if they haven't heard about it.

'Probably the least likely thing to happen is that your waters will break – it doesn't happen like in the movies.' Her exuberant descriptions matched her bright purple stockings and short spiked hair.

She went on to explain the first stage of labour, when the woman's cervix, the neck of the uterus, thins and begins to dilate. 'This stage is often the longest – especially for first births – and can last up to twenty-four hours,' she said. 'Put your feet up with a comedy and try to rest as much as possible.

'When you transition from first to second stage of labour you may feel tired, irritable, weepy, unable to control your labour. Many women throw up about then.'

In the second stage of labour the baby was pushed out. 'You might have a strong desire to push, but don't rush to push your baby out – your perineum needs to stretch gradually. This is the time to consciously relax your pelvic floor to let your baby out. Some women visualise a flower opening.'

Kass's descriptions made my head spin. I couldn't comprehend how all these things could happen inside my body. How would it feel? Would the pain be searing, like the cut of a knife, or throbbing, like a terrible migraine in your pelvis?

Back home I sifted through the contents of the goody bag we'd been given. It contained things we wouldn't need. A discount on merino sleeping bags for baby. A nappy rash cream sample. A parenting magazine. A baby growth chart. A swathe of pamphlets on ergonomic baby hammocks, 'rock and rhyme' sessions for babies held at the library, water wipes that claimed to be the world's purest. I tried to look at all these things dispassionately. I might be on a different path from the other women in the class, but who of them was taking their baby in utero to swim with whales? My Pacific getaway was happening the next week and I couldn't wait.

34 weeks

Sam, the owner of Deep Blue whale-watching tours, looked like a whale himself. He was well over six feet tall, with tree-trunk legs, a bald head, and a face dominated by teeth that looked like white pegs. I was impressed by his size and stature, but I wasn't sure he was impressed by mine. Eyeing up my pregnant form, he seemed to be mentally preparing for what to do if I went into labour on his boat.

Along with a dozen other tourists, Mandy, Amy and I had signed up for a day of watching whales, and potentially swimming with them. Several sub-groups of humpbacks migrate annually to different parts of the Pacific. The Tongan group has a route along the Kermadecs and a special song they sing only in Tonga. Mother whales calve and raise their newborns here for several months. The calves drink up to 200 litres of whale milk a day and incredibly the mothers don't eat during this time, but just live on reserves.

Mandy was fantasising about a face-to-face encounter with a hump-back, while Amy was not so sure she even wanted to get in the water. We were herded on to the boat by two guides – James from the UK and Patrick, a marine biology student from New Zealand. I asked if the whales were disturbed by the boats following them. Patrick said the boats waited for the mother and calf to approach them, and his research had shown the interactions did no harm. As the whales could move much faster than the boats, if they wanted to be left in peace they swam away.

The lecture was interrupted by a shout as someone spotted two sets of flippers emerging from the sea. 'Get ready to get in!' Sam yelled. The cold was bracing. I gasped as I tried to remember how to breathe with a snorkel and mask. It was scary being out in the deep ocean among a throng of people. We moved in the direction of the whale and her calf but they moved off. It wasn't exactly the intimate moment I'd hoped for. Next time we pulled up alongside whales, I stayed on deck with Amy and observed their magnificence from above.

Sam dropped anchor and we were served American hotdogs. As we sailed further out to sea that afternoon the wind got up and it was not long before my two hotdogs ended up overboard. Afterwards I had to sit still with my eyes fixed on the horizon for a very long time.

Back on dry land, over the next four days I loved dipping my heavily pregnant body into the clear sea on the white sand beach near our fale, watching blue starfish and tiny schools of silver fish. Tonga would always be a vibrant memory of JV's time on earth.

35 weeks

We next met Tessa at the hospital so she could give us a tour. I noticed the delivery suites were big and beige and smelt of disinfectant. They had a deceptive air of ordinariness; despite this we knew that far from ordinary events took place in them. A special facility, the Pōhutukawa Room, was reserved for women who had stillborn babies or late-term terminations. The room had some extra features – a La-Z-Boy chair, a kitchenette, a landscape painting on the wall. A Sands' Moses basket was on the table, filled with gifts. There was a folder containing ideas for making memories of your deceased baby.

'It is also the only room in the hospital with a window that can be opened,' Tessa said. This had been requested by the hospital's cultural adviser to allow the spirit of a baby who had died to fly free.

That week Jacob and Jamie's baby boy had arrived. It had been a difficult labour requiring a caesarean and a blood transfusion. I hadn't met the baby yet, and felt the need to keep a little distance. I vaguely dreaded family celebrations when his presence would remind us of the absence of our own son. This baby would receive the love and attention I would have wished for ours. I imagined he would knit his parents closer to the family in a way I would have liked for us.

That weekend I had a timely visit from an SGI Buddhist leader who was visiting from Auckland and came to our house to chant for our baby. Setsuko was Japanese and in her sixties. She had cheeks like soft dumplings that plumped up when she laughed. Her advice was just to enjoy and feel excited about our baby coming. 'You have shown him great compassion in allowing him to live and that compassion will be returned to you,' she said. 'There is nothing to worry about. We get so worried about separation but in the face of eternity it's nothing. Whatever happens, your son will be with you forever. You have changed his karma. He is teaching you, not just about this experience, but about other, greater things.'

36 weeks

I sat with half a dozen female colleagues in a French-styled salon de thé, being served tiered platters of delicate mouthfuls: quiches of duck liver paté and marmalade, smoked fish and avocado on crostini, hazelnut macaroons, chocolate truffles. I drank Casablanca, a blend of white tea and peppermint. This luxurious afternoon tea was to farewell me before I went on maternity leave but the atmosphere felt strained. I sensed these kind women didn't know what to say to me. The usual comments to a woman about to have her first baby obviously didn't apply.

Perhaps it was my fault. I could have opened up more. It had been hard to find the right moment in the staff kitchen or meeting room. Except with Sarah and one or two others, my conversations about my baby's condition had been limited to a few words. Now it didn't feel right to try and explain my journey and why I'd decided to continue the pregnancy. I was glad when Glenda from HR joked that I should get my toenails painted. 'If your feet end up in stirrups, at least you'll have something nice to look at.'

On my last day at work, most of my other colleagues didn't say goodbye, or good luck, or anything at all. I didn't really blame them. If the situation had been reversed, perhaps I myself wouldn't have reached out to a colleague I didn't know well. I was the elephant in the room, now leaving the building.

'He's a big boy, 3.5 kg already,' Dr D said as she examined the printed scan report. 'And his heart rate seems to have returned to normal.'

'Normal! That's great. Why would that be?' I asked.

Dr D didn't know. Nor did this make any difference to what Dr W had to say to us. The neonatologist was back to talk through the baby's care plan. 'I don't believe interventions would be of any use,' he said. 'I would be unwilling to attempt anything that would cause him discomfort. It would be unethical.' He underlined his position even more firmly than at the first meeting. His words seemed to allow little room for discussion.

'But, hypothetically, if you were going to do interventions, what would they be?' Roy asked. I knew what he was getting at. Dr D had hinted at the last meeting that some neonatologists might take a more proactive approach.

'As you know, surgery is not an option for your baby and there is only one possible outcome. Your baby's heart won't work as the pump that hearts are designed to be,' Dr W said.

'But what if he does live longer than expected?' I said. 'I saw a report about an ectopia cordis baby in India who was still alive after a week.'

'The problem with those news reports is that they don't detail the specifics. How severe was the ectopia cordis?'

'I don't know.'

'We also have a question for you," Dr D said. 'What role do you see Brendon Bowkett playing in the birth?' I was surprised by the slightly challenging tone in her voice.

We had been back in touch with the paediatric surgeon and he had kindly offered to be on call when the baby was born to place a dressing around his heart.

'Brendon was introduced to us by a priest we both know,' I said. 'He's offered to help and thinks his surgical skills could be useful.'

'There is only one way to cover the heart and that's with wet gauze,' Dr W said.

It seemed we'd crossed some line in hospital processes and the chain of command by making an arrangement directly with Brendon, rather than through the maternal foetal medicine team. As with the previous meetings, it was hard feeling there was no room for negotiation or to have our say as parents. Recently I'd walked past a restaurant and seen Dr D drinking wine with a group of women friends. If we'd met under different circumstances maybe we'd have been friends. But here we were playing roles: doctor and patient, the holder of knowledge and the receiver. I didn't want to antagonise the two doctors, but I was not willing to back down from doing anything that might benefit our son and the brief time we would have with him.

My mother came down for the weekend. We sat a little table in a Lebanese restaurant. 'It's going to be so hard for you to lose a child and me to lose a grandchild. I don't know how we are going to cope,' she said tearily. We had just seen a movie about a boy's life and a series of milestones our boy wouldn't have. I didn't want to let it make me sad. Similarly, I didn't want to deal with my mother's fears. I was determined to stay positive.

'Mum, you need to trust we'll be okay. You need to have faith.'

Recently I'd seen another tear-jerking film, *The Fault In Our Stars*. The protagonists were teenage lovers, both with cancer. The film explored the theme of the imperfection of our bodies – cells mutate to become cancerous, genetic encoding may be just a tiny bit wrong. It suggested such things are natural, even necessary, in this world, which is itself one great imperfect experiment. All our bodies are imperfect, and all will fail at some point. If this happens to a child or a newborn baby, we are reminded to cherish life and health all the more while we have it.

The film proposed that it is enough to be known and special to someone, even just one person, to count your life as meaningful. Using that criteria, my baby's life certainly had meaning. He was the most special person I had ever known. Despite his heart condition I felt he was perfect. It was impossible for me to think of him as anything but. Without any conscious effort I had made a deep, instinctive pact to love and accept him and his crazy heart, come what may.

37 weeks

Lying on the massage table in a warm room adorned with statues of Buddha and candles flickering, soft rhythmic music tinkling in the background, I was transported to a state of bliss. The Balinese massage was thanks to a voucher given me by colleagues at work. This is the state of mind I'd like to be in for the birth, I thought dreamily.

It was one of the first inklings I had of the sort of vibe I wanted to create for the labour. Otherwise I'd continued to draw blanks. It was just so hard to imagine how labour might be. Did contractions tear your insides apart like a plough, or did they roll through your body like waves? Would I feel better with support people on hand to rally and encourage me, or would I prefer the space and peace to go deep inside myself, with only Roy and my midwife present? I knew my mother wanted to be there, but I had a niggling fear that if she felt anxious for me and the baby I'd sense it in a minute. I decided to ask her and Amy to be on standby, with the caveat that I'd see what I felt comfortable with at the time.

I liked the idea of a water birth and Tessa was in favour of this too. In her experience water births eased the stress and pain of contractions. There was no reason she could see that being born in water would be a problem for the baby's heart.

I began to assemble some ambience-enhancing kit to take to the delivery suite: Roy's Peruvian poncho, plus the baby-sized one, to brighten the room; an aromatherapy spray; a salt crystal lamp that cast a gentle pink glow. Vicki and Joan had already given me one of the Sands' baskets. I wasn't sure exactly what we'd use from it but decided to take it too.

On stage, the handsome opera singer in a red velvet dress sung an aria from *Don Giovanni*. 'He likes the sopranos!' Roy said. He had his hand on my belly and had felt the baby flipping, turning and kicking.

Going to the opera had been Roy's idea. I'd dressed up for the first time in ages – a silver sequined top, black pants, kitten boots with a heel. The heels proved almost too much and I wished I could put my feet up, but I was pleased we'd come. We'd always associate this opera with JV now.

Roy's next brainwave was to throw a 'birth month' party. We would never have birthday parties or cakes for our baby but we could throw a party now. We decided to invite our close circle of family and friends for an afternoon tea the following Sunday.

38 weeks

'Roy, we agreed to invite twenty close friends and family. I don't even know all these people!' I'd discovered on Facebook that Roy had invited half the Latino community of Wellington to the party.

'Well, I don't know everyone you've invited either,' he retorted.

'Who is going to clean the house and do the cooking for fifty people?'

Beneath my anger at Roy was a fear that I'd feel vulnerable and exposed sharing this occasion with people I didn't know well. I hated the idea of the pressure of hosting a big party and potentially having to explain from the beginning about our baby's heart being outside of his chest and deal with their reactions.

'Well, I'll un-invite people then,' Roy said.

'That's not going to work,' I said. 'I just wish you'd stuck to what we agreed.'

Adding to my anxiety were negotiations around the purchase of the Ariki Road house. After several weeks of drilling and grinding, the re-piling was complete. The real estate agents were insisting we now had to make an offer. We offered $465,000. We were told $490,000 was the owner's bottom line. We offered $470,000. The owner dropped to $485,000. We didn't want to meet her there. Roy and I were both willing to walk away from the deal. Neither of us felt so in love with the house that we wanted to stretch ourselves too far financially.

The real estate agents became very cool once it became clear we were not going to buy the house. They wanted to know when they could begin open homes. We agreed on November 7, two weeks after the baby's due date. They said we'd be given four weeks' notice to move out. This was incorrect. We knew we were legally entitled to forty-two days' notice from the date of sale. Moving out seemed crazy given all the energy that had gone into moving in, but I felt surprisingly detached. The house just didn't seem that important compared to the pending arrival of the baby.

On Sunday Roy threw himself into organising the party. He made birthday posters in bright rainbow colours that read 'FELIZ CUMPLE JV'. He whipped up rice pudding and purple corn jelly, traditional kid's party food in Peru. My mother and Al flew down from Auckland with a suitcase full of food, including a hummingbird birthday cake Mum had made. It was adorned with bright flowers and 'Jesús Valentino' in chocolate letters.

The house quickly filled up with people. I sat on the couch and let things happen around me. The kids of a Peruvian couple I'd only just met brought along puppets and a portable stage. They'd written a show themselves and performed it in the garden. Afterwards Roy gave a speech, thanking people for coming. 'None of us know when we're going to die,' he said. 'It could happen to any of us at any moment. The same is true for our baby, but that makes loving him and each other now all the more important.'

I spoke too, saying my son had allowed me to experience a purer love than I'd ever known. I burst into tears but that was okay. In the end I didn't feel uncomfortable sharing the birth-month party with the big group who had gathered.

Roy then led everyone in a round of the song he'd been singing to JV: '¿Cómo estás Jesús Valentino? ¿Cómo estás?'

When the party was over I felt we'd celebrated our son. The difficult moments I'd feared hadn't materialised. Rather it had been a good thing to draw new people into JV's life. They would all be the keepers of his memory.

39 weeks

I decided to contact a funeral director. I hardly wanted to begin organising Jesús Valentino's funeral, yet I didn't want to be overwhelmed by the task when the time came either. I called a firm recommended by Joan and Vicki. The woman who answered sounded efficient and capable. Afterwards she sent me a summary of our conversation, and a quote that covered recording the service, catering, flowers, memorial book, service sheet, burial and cremation options, newspaper notice, music. I tried to remain detached as I looked through the long list of things to do.

I didn't feel so sanguine when Vicki called the next day. 'My husband and I made a baby coffin on the weekend, if you'd like to use it. It's constructed from a light plywood with the option of a cross for the lid.'

She sounded quite chuffed. She and her husband had set up a charitable trust to make babies' coffins and this was the first one they'd made. I was caught off guard. The coffin conjured up unwelcome images. I felt there must have been a miscommunication.

'I think we might cremate JV so I don't know if we're going to need a coffin,' I said.

'Oh, that's okay. You might still want a coffin for the service?'

'Maybe.'

I knew Vicki was being caring but I did not want to have that conversation. I could only handle thinking about my son's death in small, controlled amounts. Nor did I want to feel bad if Vicki and her husband had wasted their time constructing a coffin we wouldn't use. A few days earlier, I'd realised I wasn't ready to read a book containing poems suitable for baby funerals that she and Joan had left either. I'd thrown the book across the lounge, while screaming inside, 'Don't make me think of farewelling my baby yet, not while he is still so alive and safe, tucked up inside me.'

The next day Roy and I had a session with a woman who taught techniques for calm natural labour. She said that during her career as a doula – a birth companion or coach – she had worked in a maximum-security prison, where the labours were the longest she'd ever witnessed. 'The women didn't want to let go of their babies because they wouldn't be able to keep them after they were born. Do you feel anything like that?' she asked.

'No, not that I'm aware of,' I said.

Vicki, too, had mentioned something on the phone about women who carry babies with fatal conditions not wanting their pregnancies to end. This wasn't how I felt, or at least not consciously. I didn't want JV to feel I was anything but overjoyed that he was going to be born. I needed people to be positive about our son's life, as different as it would be from a healthy baby's. I needed people to tell us we were strong enough to walk this journey with him.

Mid-week I was frazzled and exhausted. Following the birth-month party we'd had two sessions with the doula. On Tuesday morning we'd met with Brendon to discuss his plan to dress our baby's heart when he was born. 'I've spoken with a colleague in Canada who suggested a laparoscopy bag would work best,' he said. I'd seen Julie, the homeopath, and come away with five different remedies for birth and afterwards. The one I'd chosen through blind testing for after the birth was ignatia, homeopathy's remedy for grief. The night before we'd been to a party for Amy's birthday and that night I was to celebrate my friend Carmel's fortieth. On top of this I'd been to the supermarket to buy provisions for labour: coconut water, chia-seed health food bar, organic milk and white chocolate, organic apple and feijoa juice, organic cola, iced coffee, iced mocha.

All this activity was threatening to overwhelm me. Enough, I told myself. I'd being putting pressure on myself to do all these things, when the best thing I could do to prepare for the birth was to feel unpressured. I just had one more busy day and then I could stop.

Thursday began with a date with Camilla at the kaikan. When I arrived, I found she'd invited half a dozen others and proposed we dedicate our chanting to welcoming JV to this world. Once again, through the support of these Buddhists, I felt as though a silver silk cocoon had been wrapped around me and my son.

As we were chanting an image popped into my head of a toddler crying and distraught because his parents had left the room, not understanding they were just next door. The words scrolled through my head: 'This is how it will be with JV, only the roles will be reversed. You as the parents will be distraught, but you needn't fear when he is out of sight.'

It was an idea I wanted to reflect on more, but there wasn't time that morning. We had our final appointment with Dr D and Louise. There wasn't much left to say. We ended up talking about the crossover between Catholicism and Buddhism and how both had helped us see the beauty and value in our baby's life. It was relief to finish our monthly appointments with an easy and warm interaction.

Afterwards we met Tessa in the hospital café and she introduced us to the back-up midwife she would call on if she needed extra support. Next, Roy was on the phone to the hospital chaplain, Father Patrick. Father Lyons had suggested we meet the chaplain as he would be on-hand to perform any rites we might wish for.

'I'm just in a cab coming from the airport, I'd be very happy to meet you. Can you wait ten minutes?' he said.

We waited and I was pleased we had. Father Patrick had thick hair the colour of gingernuts. He was the kind of man you could imagine telling a good yarn over a glass of red wine. I felt comfortable welcoming him into the life of our son.

By now it was five o'clock and we had to race home for a maternity photoshoot. The photographer, Billie Brook, was in her twenties, with fizzy energy and a blonde bob. We'd been put in touch with her by Sands and she was taking the photos free of charge. We posed under the 'FELIZ CUMPLE JV' birthday posters still on the wall from the party. I stood with my tummy bared in silhouette against the window. Roy put on a Peruvian poncho and held up the child-sized one he'd brought back from Peru.

'You are so photogenic,' Billie told us. We felt like superstars.

Birth

That night we had Indian takeaways. The friendly woman in a green and gold sari behind the counter told us the day was Diwali, the Indian New Year and Festival of Light. 'The council fireworks are on the weekend, but today is the real day to celebrate,' she said. As she handed over our order she winked at me and said, 'I've given you fresh rice. I know you have to be careful of these things in pregnancy.'

After dinner I idly watched television and was ready for bed by ten-thirty. As I put on my nightdress I felt a peculiar sensation. A stream of liquid was running down my legs, leaving a whitish puddle on the floor. I went to the bathroom, but before I could sit on the toilet more liquid gushed out. Could this be my waters breaking? Really – already?

'Something's happening,' I told Roy back in the lounge. 'I think my waters have broken.'

Disbelief flashed across his face. 'Right, I'm texting Tessa.'

Tessa called me back shortly afterwards. I was to try to get some sleep, and ring her in the night if labour was progressing. I texted my mother then I fell asleep.

At three in the morning I was woken by contractions. They weren't strong, more like occasional aches deep inside my belly. I began running through all the things I'd wanted to do before the birth. I wasn't sure I was ready to go into labour. I still hadn't written up my personal experience piece for the Buddhist magazine. One of the practices in Nichiren Buddhism is for people to share an experience about a challenge in their lives and reflect on how their Buddhist practice and Buddhist teachings have helped them deal with it. I'd promised Camilla I'd do this.

I got up and began writing. The words poured out of me. As the dawn began to turn the sky from black to grey, I finished the last sentences.

Whatever happens, this baby has bought me great blessings. He has dramatically deepened my Buddhist practice. He has opened my heart to others and opened others' hearts to me. He has required that I give consideration to some of life's biggest questions and mysteries. He has solidified the love between me and my partner. This baby who wears his heart on the outside has allowed me to experience the purest love I have ever known… We still have a big journey ahead of us, my son and me, but I am very excited to meet him. I can't say why my baby's heart has grown in the way it has, but I know there is a reason. I look forward to loving him and learning from him as the mystery continues to unfold.

My writing task out of the way, I was ready for the contractions to start again, but inconveniently they'd subsided. At six-thirty I got a text from my mother. She hadn't messed around. She was on her way to the airport and would soon arrive in Wellington.

When Roy woke up he was cross that I had not stayed in bed. 'You were supposed be resting, conserving your energy.' It was true. I was tired. My early start to the day was catching up with me.

Around ten o'clock my mother arrived, guns blazing. Straight away I felt fussed over and began to bristle. I wanted to be able to potter about, undistracted by the world around me. Realising I wanted space, she left to unpack at the place where she was staying.

Through Friday afternoon and evening, contractions came and went, fickle as the wind. When they came, it was as if a wide belt around my pelvis was being squeezed and I was engulfed by the feeling. Around midnight, they began to come more often, about every ten minutes. Roy had lit the fire in the lounge. I lit candles and placed affirmations written on pastel-coloured paper on the coffee table and window sills. Everything felt ready for labour to progress. I was good to go. But then the contractions stopped again.

Saturday dawned bright and sunny. At lunchtime Amy came over with an enormous white protea, a flower fit for a prince. We walked up and down our steps and along the road. I felt other-worldly, my mind and body completely preoccupied with the labour. The contractions still weren't coming fast, but they were coming. I shut my eyes and breathed into them, making a sing-song note as I exhaled. I ate some strawberries for lunch. I had two more baths. Tessa visited and gave me a homeopathic remedy to speed up labour but it didn't seem to have an effect.

She called later in the afternoon. 'I've spoken to Dr D and they'd like you to come in. They're worried about how much time has passed since your waters broke.' There was apparently a risk of infection if your waters broke too long before the onset of active labour. 'One option would be to induce you this afternoon.'

I wanted to avoid both antibiotics and induction. I'd read that in labour the induction process messed with the body's natural cascade of hormones and put more stress on the baby, sometimes affecting its heart rate. Antibiotics kill the beneficial bacteria in your gut and the birth canal, to which you want the baby to be exposed.

'Can we wait a bit longer? I might go into labour properly overnight.'

Tessa said induction could be held off until the next day and that I didn't have to have antibiotics yet if I showed no sign of fever or high pulse rate. 'But how about we transfer you from home to hospital so they can keep an eye on you?'

At the delivery suite there was a shiny gift bag filled with baby clothes. It had been left by Roy's former flatmates, Nacho, Olga, Karen and Nick. I was very moved. No one else had given us clothes for the baby, thinking we wouldn't need them. Tessa had also bought flowers and gifts – coffee syrup and portable coffee cups.

'The hospital staff really want me to give you antibiotics,' Tessa said. I was still reluctant but I agreed to have a line put in the back of my hand in case I needed them intravenously later. The vein was hard to find and my hand ended up sore and bruised.

By the evening my contractions had vanished. I was exhausted. It was now coming up to forty-eight hours since my waters had broken and although I'd been dealing with the demands of labour I had little to show for it. It was like waiting on a platform for a train that has been indefinitely delayed. I was feeling disappointed and defeated.

I agreed to be induced in the morning. In the meantime I took Tessa's suggestion to take a sleeping pill so I could at least get a good night's rest beforehand. The sleeping pill did not have the desired effect. Not long after I'd taken it the contractions began again. I got up and began bouncing on the swiss ball.

Roy tried to sleep while I commenced a strange routine of swaying my hips, bouncing on the swiss ball, and sitting on the toilet. After a while I pushed the bell for the duty midwife.

'I took a sleeping pill but it seems to have made my contractions start again.'

'Sometimes that happens as your muscles relax. Would you like me to see how far dilated you are? I'd need to give you antibiotics first though.'

Apparently internal examinations increase your likelihood of infection and this midwife didn't like the fact I hadn't had any yet. The drip was fed into the line in my hand.

'You're the strong silent type, aren't you?' the midwife said as she examined me. It turned out I was already seven centimetres dilated. 'I'll call your midwife to come back in,' she said.

By midnight Tessa was back and running the birth pool for me, but when I got in it felt much too hot and I got straight back out. Roy was awake now but feeling feverish himself. Four hours later I began pushing. I wanted to be sitting, so a birth stool was found. The pushes took all my concentration and energy. I squeezed the life out of Roy's hand. At one point I bit him so hard I drew blood.

'Maybe you should tell Mum to come to the hospital now,' I said. Seconds later the door opened and my mother was in the room, carrying the Sands' basket. I got a huge fright, having thought she was at home. I didn't know if my baby would be born alive and the basket was a reminder he might not be. I was also furious with Roy for inviting her to wait outside the delivery suite without telling me.

'Roy, that was my decision, not yours. Say sorry, say sorry!' I yelled.

I had now been pushing as if my life depended on it for three hours. Ordinarily the pushing phase lasts an hour at the most. 'I think we might give you syntocinon to speed up contractions,' Tessa said. Syntocinon is an artificial form of oxytocin.

I was relocated on to the bed. I wasn't sure if I liked the idea of this drug, and sure enough as it pulsed through me I feel overwhelmed and out of control. The contractions were now like breakers hitting me, dragging me under, instead of waves swelling up inside me. I ran out of courage. Nothing seemed to be happening. My midwife's cheers weren't so encouraging anymore. Hope drained from me. I had no more energy.

'I don't think I can do it. I think I need some help.'

'There are two options: the pudendal block or the epidural,' Tessa said.

'I'll take your recommendation,' I snapped. I was in no state for conscious thought.

Tessa insisted I say what I wanted. I said pudendal block.

'Do you realise we'll turn the lights on?' she said. By then I didn't care.

It seemed to take forever for the doctor to arrive and the equipment to be bought into the room. There was some pain as a needle went in. Then there was relief. Tessa also offered me nitrous oxide to inhale, which I accepted. The doctor seemed to be slicing my vagina. I was surprised but not particularly worried to note this. There was still pushing, yes, but also tugging from something called a ventouse cup.

And then there was a baby.

Day 1, Sunday

Jesús Valentino Costilla Gilkison was born on his due date, October 26, 2014, at 6.58 a.m. He weighed 3.6 kilograms, 7.9 pounds. I had laboured for fifty-six hours.

He was placed on my chest, a wet, warm, squirmy bundle. Immediately the sharp distress and flailing desperation of my long labour evaporated. The world became soft and diffuse, awash in warm amber light. No longer was I an incoherent and slightly crazed woman. I was in a state of rapture.

'Hello, my darling, aren't you amazing? You are here, you are here. It's so wonderful to see you.'

'Hijito, we love you so much.' Roy wept. He took off his shirt so he could cradle our son against his bare skin.

My legs were up in stirrups and I was being prodded inside. I was vaguely aware of Tessa saying something about the placenta still needing to be birthed. It didn't matter. Nothing really mattered. My baby was born. My baby was alive. We'd met him. He was breathing. He cried.

Later I would read Tessa's notes:

Baby Jesus Valentino arrived today, his due date, at 0658 after a huge effort by his Mum Emma and support team. He was assisted out with ventouse and straight up to Emma, skin to skin. Welcomed by family and friends, Jesus weighs 3630g. His beautiful heart he wears on his chest but it has been covered for cuddle time. Some sucks at the breast and a lick of colostrum.

Brendon Bowkett came into the room. 'Hi,' I said breezily. 'This is our friend Brendon, darling. He's going to cover your heart.' This was recorded on video by Amy, who had been waiting outside the delivery suite. When I watched the footage later, I was impressed by the bonhomie I mustered, as if Brendon had just stepped in for a cup of tea.

JV was taken from my chest and over to a table where his exposed heart was covered and sealed with a plastic surgical bag. On top of this a wodge of padding was placed. Around the padding, bandages were wrapped. I don't even remember seeing his heart before it was covered. It didn't seem an important detail compared to meeting him.

A few minutes later, to my surprise, Father Lyons walked into the room. Unbeknownst to me, he had been called at four a.m. and had also been waiting outside the delivery suite, to baptise our baby. I was now being stitched up – the slicing feeling I'd felt at the end of the labour was an episiotomy – and my legs were still up in the stirrups. All of this would have been in full view as Father Lyons walked to the side of the bed but he seemed to take this in his stride.

He had a styrofoam cup filled with water, blessed by him, to perform the baptism. I remember seeing red flames in the room. Later, in a photo, I noticed there was a vase of red flowers on the bedside table, so I may have been still coming down from the nitrous oxide gas. Father Lyons read the prayer for the day:

> Through the loving compassion of our God
> The dawn from on high shall break upon us
> To shine on those who dwell in darkness
> In the shadow of death, guide our feet unto the way of peace.

The words felt appropriate. Hadn't my son been teaching me much about loving compassion? And, yes, in the shadow of death we'd had to find peace. Father Lyons would tell his congregation at mass that morning that he had met baby Jesús who had descended from on high at dawn.

'I've spoken to the paediatrician and you're to feed baby once every two hours with two mls of expressed milk or formula or water. We've got to make sure he's well hydrated,' said Harriet, the duty midwife. She had come to see us in the Pōhutukawa Room, where we'd been moved. Harriet was young, with freckles and a bouncing ponytail, but her upbeat, direct manner inspired confidence.

'It'll be easier for him to be fed by syringe than to suckle. Breastfeeding is the most energy-intensive thing a baby does and we don't want to put him under any extra pressure,' she explained. She had bought us a handful of small slim syringes in plastic wrappers to drip milk or water into JV's mouth. She showed me how to squeeze droplets of milk from my breasts and siphon them up with a syringe.

'No one else has really told us how we should care for our son,' I said, grateful for Harriet's practical advice. 'No one thought we would have this time. We didn't even think to buy nappies.' My mother had gone out to get some.

Harriet looked concerned. 'I'll see if the on-duty neonatologist can come to talk to you.'

In the hospital notes Harriet wrote:

1400 Welcome to the Pohutukawa Room little man. Crying and alert. Looking for food. Hand expressed 0.5mls and given by Mum via syringe. Appears content and comfortable. …

1500 Baby tucked up in bed with Mummy … Trying to sort possible discharge plan. As baby was unexpected to survive no plan was made for postnatal palliative care … Paediatrician to come and review situation and help develop a plan. Suggested currently: to maintain comfort; keep warm;

feed 2 hourly with 2mls expressed breast milk or H_2O to help maintain hydration; to start morphine or pain relief if baby in pain or unsettled.

For most of the afternoon JV slept peacefully in my arms, wrapped in a cream woollen blanket given by my father and stepmother. Every time I looked at him I was suffused with warm feelings. The palm of his left hand rested against the side of his face and his head tilted slightly, making me think of a philosopher in contemplation. He had cheeks like plump pillows, a pointy chin, and fine hair like lines of black ink. His smell was a sweet single note. When his brow furrowed, I gently stroked out the creases with my little finger. When he opened his eyes, they were like shining black opals, tiny planets from a far-off universe. I thought I might see a hybrid blend of Roy and me yet he seemed his own person, with a distinct presence from the get-go. Where had this little being come from, I wondered. Through what series of miracles had his soul travelled here?

Later that day we had a champagne toast with Mum, Al, who had flown in from Auckland, Phoebe and Luke who had flown in from Christchurch, Maggie, Dad, my sister Eleanor, Amy and Camilla. I was deeply tired and in other circumstances would have felt overwhelmed by this big group, the rare mixing of the two halves of my family. But with my baby asleep and swaddled in my arms, all was well in the world. This was love without a smidgeon of ambiguity.

Day 2, Monday

At six-thirty a.m. JV was awake. I held him in my arms and fed him droplets of milk, which he lapped up like a happy kitten. I couldn't believe it. Yesterday hadn't been a dream after all. My baby was alive.

At three in the morning he'd been awake and crying. We'd rocked him, fed him and still he'd cried. We had no idea why until finally it dawned on us to check his nappy. Sure enough there was a poo. Our baby had pooed! We weren't mentally prepared for such things. Yet here we were, bumbling through, getting a crash course in caring for a newborn. While fathers are not usually allowed to stay overnight in the ward, they'd let us fold out the La-Z-Boy into a single bed and Roy had slept under our poncho from Peru.

At seven-thirty there was a knock on the door. An orderly delivered a breakfast tray of wholemeal toast, butter and jam, stewed fruit, rice bubbles and milk. I tucked into the plain food as if it was a sumptuous spread. At eight Mum arrived with a tray of takeaway coffees and I guzzled down an espresso, hoping the caffeine in my breast milk wouldn't be too much for the baby.

'A bit of a fracas has erupted. Ordinarily NICU [neonatal intensive care unit] looks after babies with special needs, but they haven't been delegated responsibility as they didn't think JV would be alive this long.' Tessa was explaining the situation. 'The midwives on this ward don't feel confident about managing his care… The hospital's been caught on the back foot.'

This was outlined in the hospital notes I later requested.

1100 … we are concerned that 'baby Jesus' has not been admitted to Neonatal Unit for care from NICU nurses and continuation of palliative care. Agreed to following plan:

- To be admitted to NICU and on leave to Pods
- Will have a visit from a neonatal nurse or paediatrician every shift
- To sort out homecare and follow-on care tomorrow

… they are aware that this is out of our scope of practice and concerned that we may miss the point when the baby needs morphine or further input/ care. Therefore needs neonatal nurse input.

At midday, as the hospital machine lurched into motion, we met Tisha, a community neonatal nurse. 'What a lovely wee boy. You're a battler, aren't you?' she said to JV. Tisha had a broad friendly face and wide arms you could imagine wrapping you in a bear hug.

I told her we'd noticed our baby's skin colour changing. Sometimes it had a blueish tinge and other times it was pale pink.

'That's what we'd expect,' she said. 'It's harder work for him to circulate blood around his body and you may notice he'll become a bit bluer if he's been crying.'

'Do you think it's easier for him to breathe if he is upright, rather than lying down?' I'd got the sense that was what JV preferred. His breathing was fast and shallow and the beating of his heart inside the plastic colostomy bag was quite audible.

'Yes, I think you're right. Keep him upright or at a forty-five-degree angle. Over time JV's lungs may fill up with fluid. If they do, you'll hear his breath become raspy, he may have little choking episodes as he tries to bring up mucous. You may also find at some point he gets irritable and can't settle. Babies in discomfort often squirm and wiggle like puppies trying to find a comfortable spot. Watch out for his hands and feet getting cold too.'

Tisha spoke directly, but with a tone that suggested there was nothing to get flustered about, so I didn't find the conversation distressing. My baby's comfort was my utmost wish and I felt Tisha, as she told us how best to look after him, was an ally.

'Have you thought about going home?' she asked next.

I was taken aback. Nothing we'd been told in our meetings with doctors had suggested we prepare for having JV at home, and we had none of the things we'd need, such as a bassinet, baby bath, or nappy changing station. Our house was cold and there were ninety-five steps up to it. Most of all I didn't want to be far away from the midwives and doctors who could help with JV's care, who would know if he needed pain relief. My knee-jerk reaction was a firm no.

I would later read in the hospital notes that we'd been expected to leave.

1515 Dr K and myself went to 4North to meet Emma, Roy and baby Jesus. Jesus lying comfortably in bed with dad – blue in colour but no noticeable increase in work of breathing. Tisha … (Homecare) had already visited and outlined the process for getting the family to go home in the next day or two.

After the initial hands-off approach to our care, we began to see a lot of people. Two female doctors arrived to see us in their blue scrubs, one very small and the other large, like Laurel and Hardy. I didn't know how they fitted in. It was as if a conveyor belt deposited a medical professional in our room every couple of hours. Twice a day, with each change of shift, the midwife assigned to us would come and introduce herself. Then there were staff from the neonatal unit. Dr D visited with a registrar. Tessa was still visiting too.

It was a relief when night fell and our room became quiet. The salt lamp I'd bought from home cast a soft glow. Around the lamp I'd hung the koru pounamu pendant my Mum and Al had given JV. I happily watched our son as he suckled on a bottle. Roy sat next to me, dabbing the drops of milk that escaped from JV's mouth with a muslin cloth. When JV had fallen asleep in my arms I sent an email from my phone, announcing his arrival.

Dear friends,

Our darling son Jesús Valentino was born on Sunday morning at 6.58am, weighing 3.63 kilograms. My waters broke late Thursday night, so it was a long labour, but of course so worth it.

JV is doing better than any of the medical specialists expected. His heart is still outside his chest, but he is feeding well, crying when his nappies are changed & making his Mum and Dad very proud. We are cherishing this time we have.

Thanks for all your love & support – our son has clearly benefitted from it! If you text or email & I don't reply it's just because there's a lot going on at the hospital, but I really appreciate all the wishes that have been sent our way.

Love, Emma, Roy & JV

Day 3, Tuesday

The midwife on duty discovered pus on the sheet where JV had been sleeping. His dressing would have to be reassessed, she told us. Dr W would come to do the dressing change.

Roy and I looked at each other and shook our heads. 'Does it have to be Dr W?' Roy said. 'Couldn't Brendon change his dressings?'

At this point we had little trust in Dr W, who had dismissed our questions and said categorically that we would have only a little time with our son if he survived the birth. Now the opposite seemed to be happening.

Dr W, Brendon and Tisha all arrived. JV was laid in a hospital bassinet with clear Perspex sides. Roy and I stood at the head, each giving our son a little finger to grip. I tried to send all the love I had down through my little finger to reassure JV that everything was okay.

The outer bandage was unwound and the padding beneath it removed.

'¿Cómo estás, Jesús Valentino? ¿Cómo estás? Muy bien.' Roy began singing the song he had sung to JV during my pregnancy. Our little one was wide-eyed but he stayed remarkably calm. I tried not to watch the dressing change. When I glanced down it was like witnessing open-heart surgery, only there was no anaesthetic, no sterile operating theatre. The area around JV's beating heart was cleaned and his heart was sealed inside a new plastic colostomy bag. This was taped down to his chest. On top of this was a new wodge of padding, and around the padding a fresh bandage.

The hospital notes outlined the mechanics of the dressing change – instructions for whoever would do it next.

Care of external heart: Heart in colostomy bag on chest. Only change if seal broken and fluid leaking or if smells. Does not need irrigating or any other fluids in the bag as sealed, serous membrane and body temp will keep moist. Dressing: [supplies in bag in Homecare Office]. Remove old bag gently.
- May need to use 'remove wipes' to loosen bag from skin in some areas
- Put collodion on skin round base of tissue/blood vessel stalk emanating from chest but do not let heart tissue touch the collodion.
- Colostomy bag is cut to about 40cm
- Place the colostomy bag over heart and seal the bag onto skin
- Then white tape from roll put over colostomy bag and onto skin to protect heart from being moved and to stop bag rubbing on chin.

'Even though JV is doing much better than expected, there is still no chance of surgery.' Brendon was speaking to us quietly after the dressing change. Perhaps he'd been asked to reiterate this on the basis we were more likely to believe it if it came from him.

'I wanted to hear my son cry and Emma wanted to see his eyes open. We've been given that and that already feels like a miracle,' Roy told him.

We weren't harbouring any false illusions about our son's prognosis, though witnessing the dressing change and getting glimpses of JV's fragile, exposed heart had made me feel in awe of how well he was doing. His appetite was so good I couldn't express breast milk fast enough to keep up and was now supplementing it with formula. When he wanted milk, his mouth formed an 'O' shape and his lips moved in and out.

Mum and Phoebe had gone on a shopping expedition and come back with merino gowns and hats and a baby sling. A hedge of cards lined a cabinet in our room and behind them bouquets of flowers bloomed in vases. We had begun receiving visitors and my friend Angie had flown from Auckland to meet JV in person. I'd received also dozens of replies to the email I'd sent:

Welcome beautiful baby Jesus! I cried big fat tears of joy when I read your message last night and again when I saw these beautiful photos this morning. What a brave, beautiful, blessed baby boy Jesus is.

Welcome little determined Jesus Valentino, well done you for such an epic labour, and what incredibly special time this must be. Gorgeous pictures!

You look so proud and so beautiful and soft and tender. JV is so gorgeous!! What a little hero he is!! I am in awe of you all and so admiring of the heroic way you are all managing this situation.

The night before, Roy had had a dream about taking JV to a mass at Sacred Heart Cathedral. 'We were dressed all in white,' he reported. 'So was everyone in the church. Dr W, Tisha, Brendon, Camilla, Jimi, my family, your family were all in the congregation. Children were going up to be blessed and we took JV too. I felt so happy. Then the dream moved to another church, a wooden one where we were chanting nam-myoho-renge-kyo. Maybe we could take JV to mass?'

I smiled, indulging him, thinking in my head: As if we could. This time we were having with JV was beyond my wildest dreams, but I knew it wouldn't last.

Before I went into labour I'd had a slight cough. This had been getting progressively worse and keeping me awake during the precious times when JV slept. Thomasin came to visit and brought a bottle of cough medicine, but it contained codeine to which I react badly. My mother went to the pharmacy but bought a decongestant instead of a cough suppressant and it made me cough more. At eleven that night, desperate for something to help me sleep, I made an SOS call to Phoebe, who agreed to pick up another brand at the supermarket. Our roles had completely reversed from the days when she was a child and I was the teenager who looked after her.

Dr C, the registrar who delivered JV and did my episiotomy, unexpectedly came to check on me. When Phoebe arrived with a bottle of Irish Moss cough medicine, the doctor explained the official hospital line that cough medicines do not improve recovery times and can mask symptoms.

'I know, but I just really need something to help me sleep well,' I said.

'Okay, I'll make sure there are no contraindications with the decongestant you've taken,' Dr C said. She took both bottles and reappeared twenty minutes later. 'The good news is that the medicines are okay together. The bad news is that I broke the bottle of Irish Moss,' she said sheepishly.

I was aghast. The Irish Moss was my last chance of a good night's sleep. The doctor agreed to see if she could find some other cough medicine in the hospital. The bottle she brought back had codeine in it. I swallowed some but with the predictable outcome: my thoughts raced and I couldn't sleep during the short time JV did. Later I would see the funny side of this debacle.

Day 4, Wednesday

During the night JV was unsettled and crying. We thought it might be wind – I'd eaten cabbage with dinner and a clove of garlic to try and get rid of my cough. Or was his heart causing him discomfort? It was impossible to know what was regular newborn behaviour and what was a symptom of ectopia cordis. He didn't like to sleep lying down flat. Every time we tried to put him, sleeping, into his bassinet he'd wake in minutes, but cradled in our arms he was peaceful.

'Maybe someone should always be holding him if that's what he prefers,' I said to Roy in the depths of the night. That meant someone had to be awake all night. Roy and I took turns but I was now completely exhausted. I was beginning to come apart at the seams.

It was a relief when my mother arrived at the hospital at eight in the morning bearing takeaway coffee. I handed JV to her and drifted back into a half-sleep. I wondered how to find the energy to keep going. In my mind I travelled to Mexico and saw La Virgen de Guadalupe in her green robe studded with gold stars. La Virgen is Mexico's Virgin Mary, but some believe she also represents an Aztec goddess of life and death, fecundity and destruction. I sat up and said to Phoebe, who had just arrived, 'Do you think you could get my Guadalupe statue next time you go back to our house?'

At that moment Roy walked into the room. He'd been Skyping with his parents in Lima. 'Guess what? My Mum was just telling me how she has been praying to Guadalupe. She printed out those pictures you sent her when she was sick.' When Roy's mother had been unwell the year before, I'd photographed my retablos, devotional paintings from Mexico with Guadalupe in the centre.

Later that morning Roy burst excitedly into our room. 'Paula, the real estate agent, called. Guess what? The owner is now willing to drop her price to meet ours. We can buy our house.' I found it hard get my head around this. The realm of house-buying seemed distant and unimportant compared with caring for JV. Today Mum and I were going to give him his first bath, in advance of another photo shoot that afternoon with the lovely Billie Brook.

We filled a plastic tub with warm water and dipped in JV's legs. His body tensed on feeling the water. His mouth formed an unsure squiggle and he wriggled his gangly pink-purple limbs. His skin was still speckled with the remnants of his birth. Mum sponged him with a flannel. I sang 'Old MacDonald Had A Farm' and bit by bit he relaxed.

When Billie arrived we set up shots with JV wrapped in a family shawl hand-crocheted by my grandmother and lying on the poncho from Peru. We posed with him in our arms, the statue of Guadalupe in the background, and rose petals on the shawl.

2000 Jesus continues to be lovingly cared for by family. Tisha reports he looks better than this morning.

2140 Being cuddled by Aunt. No problems reported. Parents report Jesus extra hungry this evening and tolerating EBM/formula well.

Given our new policy that JV would live his life always held in someone's arms, Phoebe had offered to stay with us until midnight. Her support, along with my mother's, had been incredible. She sang softly to him:

This little light of mine, I'm gonna let it shine,
This little light of mine, I'm gonna let it shine,
Let it shine, let it shine, let it shine.

I'd never heard this gospel song before but it was perfect for JV, shining his little light against the odds. Every time I looked at him my heart swooned. I'd read about a curious phenomenon that happens when mothers and babies interact. Researchers at the Bar Ilan University in Israel found that, simply by looking at each other and smiling, a mother and her baby could synchronise their heartbeats to within milliseconds. The heart produces a stronger electromagnetic field than any other organ, 5,000 times greater than the field generated by the brain. The researchers theorised that it might be this electromagnetic field that allowed mothers' and babies' hearts to synchronise. I was enchanted by thought the heart really was the organ of love.

Day 5, Thursday

By the fifth day of Jesús Valentino's life we'd begun to wonder if the doctors who told us our baby's heart was incompatible with life had got it wrong. JV got hungrier by the day. We'd exchanged drip-feeding him by syringe with giving him a bottle, to which he would latch on like a hungry mollusc.

'Why do you think he is doing so much better than expected?' we asked Dr W.

'I've been consulting widely,' he said. 'I think he is using extra vessels between the lungs and circulatory system to transport oxygen, vessels that are ordinarily used only when a baby is in utero.'

'Could it be that his heart wasn't as malformed as they thought when we had the appointment in Auckland at nineteen weeks?' Roy said. 'Maybe his heart grew differently after that, or the scan images weren't clear enough.' It was the diagnosis that JV's heart had defects other than the ectopia cordis that had ruled out surgery.

'I've been in touch with Dr Gentles at Auckland Hospital. He said he wouldn't assess JV again until he was three months old, and even then he wouldn't propose surgery.'

'Is there any other way JV's heart could be assessed again?'

'It would have to be a CT scan, which would require putting JV under anaesthetic and that could be too much for his heart,' Dr W said. 'He'd be inside the machine alone, away from you for thirty minutes. We don't have the machine here. He'd have to go to Auckland, which would mean a plane ride, possibly only one parent aboard, and again this could be the moment he passed. I don't think you'd want that.'

It was a long list of nos. 'It's hard for us to trust the diagnosis when we were told so categorically we wouldn't have this time,' I said.

'We're asking you to open your heart to our baby, to think of any possibilities that you might not have thought of,' Roy said. He had tears in his eyes.

Afterwards Dr W changed the dressing again. It was the same routine with gauze, plastic gloves, scissors. As before, I averted my eyes, knowing if I saw what was happening I might feel scared, and if I felt scared JV would know and be scared too. He cried more than the first time. We sang '¿Cómo estás, Jesús Valentino?', round after round. We also slipped a syringe of sucrose into his mouth. 'It's like cocaine for babies,' Dr W said. JV's pupils dilated with the sugar high.

That afternoon Dr W came back. 'We can do a scan of JV's heart in about ten minutes,' he said breathlessly. He'd thought of an alternative to the CT scan. They would try using ultrasound scanning equipment.

Shortly afterwards a big ultrasound machine was wheeled in by a radiographer. The plan was to take off the outer bandages and place the scanning probe over the plastic colostomy bag that enclosed JV's heart.

'I'm not getting a clear picture. There are air bubbles inside the colostomy bag,' the radiographer said after she began scanning. The only answer was to take off the colostomy bag and place the ultrasound probe directly on JV's heart. Doing this flew in the face of instinct. Organs shouldn't be exposed, much less touched directly with a scanning instrument. Yet this is exactly what happened.

JV kept looking at us with wide eyes. We sang to him, naming all the important people in his life, summoning their presence. '¿Cómo estás, Father Lyons? ¿Cómo estás, your grandparents in Peru? ¿Cómo estás, Camilla and Jimi?' When I wasn't singing, my teeth were clenched. The sight of our small baby's beating heart, exposed on his chest, pulsating like a pink fish, being touched by a probe, was almost too much to bear.

When the scanning was finished, JV's heart was sealed and bandaged again and the machine wheeled from the room. With the hoopla over, we decided to go for a walk. It was a sunny spring day and the first time I'd been out of the hospital since arriving in the delivery suite five days before. Being outside with JV in Roy's arms felt peculiar and disorientating. The sky was so blue. The grass was so green. Everything looked so big. I realised my eyes had become accustomed to focusing only at close range. 'I really want to lie down on the grass,' I said. The only grass available was a small verge next to the carpark. I must have been an odd sight for passers-by as I lay with the sun on my face and fresh air filling my lungs.

When we got back to the ward, a team was huddled outside our room, waiting to talk to us – Dr W, Tisha, Father Patrick, Tessa. They'd been wondering where we'd got to and seemed quite fidgety. When we sat down, Dr W said, 'The scans have confirmed what was seen at nineteen weeks. Jesús has a hyperplastic left heart, transposition of the great arteries, pulmonary atresia, a large VSD, and possibly a common atrium.'

I interrupted Dr W and asked my mother to take JV and sit with him by the window. I didn't want him to feel my reaction to this news. Dr W then drew a picture for us and wrote down long words. The prognosis remained the same. JV's condition was fatal. He might survive for a bit, but not much longer.

'His heart doubled in size from Sunday to Tuesday and is about a third bigger again today,' continued Dr W. 'The tissue around the stalk of cardiac vessels are more swollen and the blood vessels themselves look more fragile.'

While we weren't being told anything new, that morning we'd boarded a rollercoaster, hoping for a miracle that would tell us our baby was a candidate for surgery after all, that his heart could be put back in his chest. He wasn't and it couldn't. Now we were spiralling downwards again.

Dr W wrote in his notes:

I am extremely concerned that the tissue of the vascular pedicle may become eroded, especially if infection takes hold. There is a risk of significant bleed as a terminal event for the baby. MW and NICU staff are aware and understand that this would be a terminal event, managed with pressure locally/gauze padding etc. ... All questions at this stage have at this stage been answered. The family understand that care for Jesus is purely palliative and that we cannot give precise prognosis re: life expectancy or cause of demise. However, within 7 – 10 days is a reasonable time to work from.

After the meeting I entered a strange state: distressed, numb, overwhelmed, and wracked with coughs. Most disturbingly, I found I didn't want to hold my baby anymore. It was as if my strength had evaporated. 'I'm scared I won't be able to look after JV properly like this,' I wept.

Mum bought fish and chips for our dinner. They were meant to be a treat, but they tasted greasy and disgusting. Dad and Maggie were supposed to visit between five and seven. They arrived at seven-fifteen and I sent them away, hating myself for it but unable to face company. I wanted to go home and close the door on the whole experience. Perhaps the cost of watching my baby's heart being scanned today had been too great.

Hours later, in the quiet of the night, my emotions eased. Phoebe held my sleeping darling. She'd received a text from broadcaster John Campbell, for whose family she nannied. She'd asked for the week off work to stay in Wellington and had told John and his family about her nephew. He had texted:

Dearest Phoebe, a note to send you our love down there in Wellie, as your sis and your family, and you, all try to cope with this incredibly difficult time. Sometimes things don't make any sense. My sister lost a baby, who survived the birth and drifted away in the hours afterwards. Always seemed to me to defy any semblance of what a parent should be expected to go through. Terrible. She now has a daughter who lights up their world. It doesn't mitigate their loss, or make it better or easier, but there was something after it. Something beautiful. Sometimes things too precious to be lost, are lost. As cruel and unjust and terrible as that is. And all you can do is love each other. And make sure (somehow) that hope isn't lost then, too. Please send our love to your sis. And hugs. And our knowledge that good things can and do follow even the saddest and hardest of times. Believe that. Because it's true. Love to you all.

At midnight I took over from Phoebe. I decided that rather than dwell on all the scan had revealed was wrong with JV's heart, I needed to focus on how well he was doing. Fortified by chocolate panettone, I tapped out an email to friends and family.

October 31, 12.16am (night shift)
Wonderful people,
Thank you for your beautiful words & loving wishes for me, Roy & JV. Please excuse the bulk reply. This baby – currently asleep in my arms – is keeping us very busy.

Today we went for a walk in the sun with JV. He did a fair bit of suckling. Got wind. Tried out some of the flash new outfits he's been given. Held our fingers with his hand. Just like a regular newborn! He was also the bravest baby in all of Wellington during two heart exams.

While JV's life force is awesome, the latest scan showed up the same problems. So it's a case of loving this time day by day. Roy says everyone's prayers for JV have already been answered by the amazing time we've had so far.

Amor, love & muchas gracias,
Xxx Emma, Roy & J. Valentino

Day 6, Friday

'We're planning an outing on Sunday,' I told Camilla and Jimi. 'We're going to take JV to mass, and I want to stop at the kaikan too.' Overnight I'd had my first four-hour block of sleep since JV was born and I was feeling much better. I was still tired but in a lethargic way, rather than adrenaline-filled. I'd turned a corner from the despair of the day before.

The plan, which I'd dismissed as unrealistic when Roy suggested it earlier, was now taking shape. Sunday was the monthly World Peace Chanting meeting. Tisha had said she would come with us. Dr W had given her permission.

The Pōhutukawa Room now barely contained us. The kitchenette was overflowing with chocolate, cakes, and scones baked by my father. Our clothes were piled up in the corners. A collection of gifts, cards and flowers had amassed on a shelf.

'I wonder if you might be more comfortable at Mary Potter Hospice,' Dr W said when he visited that day. The hospice was just a block away from the hospital. I wasn't sure, but I agreed to have a look.

Dr W's letter to the head of the hospice read:

Dear Brian,

Thank you for agreeing to help with the care of this baby and his family. Jesus was born at full term, following an antenatal diagnosis of complex congenital heart disease. His constellation of problems is unfortunately not amenable to any surgical or curative management. … We recognise that this is an unusual and complex case and it gives some unique challenges with regard to patient care. We (NICU) are very happy to maintain shared care with this patient and via home care will continue to manage dressing changes and whatever other assistance is required.

Dr W had also brought us a gift. 'I told my children about JV and they wanted to give him something.' It was a book called *Just You and Me*, about a baby gosling and mother goose who were looking for shelter from the storm. The little gosling didn't want to shelter with any of the other animals they encountered – badgers, ducks, hedgehogs. He just wanted to snuggle up alone with his mother.

I was touched by this gesture. Despite the rocky start to our relationship, I knew now that Dr W was doing everything he could to help us.

When he left I returned to expressing milk, the first thing I did whenever there was a gap between visitors. I would have liked JV to have only my breast milk, but we were still supplementing it with formula to keep up with demand. It was deeply satisfying to watch JV slurp down his milk and see the look of blissful satiation on his face when he finished. On this day he was wearing little green booties and a white gown patterned with green farm animals.

Day 7, Saturday

The Mary Potter Hospice was across the road from the hospital. I was surprised how light, airy and happy it felt. I'd had visions of suffering elderly sitting inertly in the kinds of stuffy lounges you find in retirement homes. Instead there were colourful mosaics on the walls, vases of fresh flowers, and staff with a spring in their step.

We were given a tour. There was a large 'family room' to hang out in, with comfy couches and a kitchen. If we came to stay we would have a private room with big windows, and French doors that led to a patio. 'Imagine just being able to step outside with JV and sit in the sun,' I murmured. What's more there would be a proper bed for Roy. Counselling, music therapy and massages were also on offer.

'I think we should do it,' I said to Roy as we walked back to the hospital.

'Me too,' he said.

A block away, a Saturday morning fruit and vegetable market was in full swing. I sat on a bench while Roy got us roti wraps for lunch. It was strange to see people bustling about and living their lives. We had needed to stay cocooned in the Pōhutakawa Room for the past week, but now it was time to venture out into the world again.

Francis had flown from Tauranga to see us. She handed me a small, thin, white, heart-shaped shell she'd dived deep in the ocean to find.

That afternoon the visits continued. I wanted to see people and show off my baby, but it took energy. I felt I had to entertain, make chit-chat, introduce people to each other. A couple of times people asked when my baby would wake up. Perhaps they were hungry for a moment with him. The thought made me bristle protectively.

When everyone finally left I got up from the bed to stretch my legs. JV was sleeping in my arms. Suddenly warm liquid poured down my legs. I passed JV to Roy and went to the bathroom, where I discovered I was bleeding badly. I called for Mum, who pushed the button on the wall. A midwife arrived and helped mop up the blood. There were two big clots. Could they have accumulated while I was sitting in the bed? I was shaking and scared and weak.

'It's not uncommon to pass blood clots post-birth,' the midwife said. 'Have something to eat and see if you can get some rest.'

Roy and I lay on the bed, with JV propped up on a pillow between us. These moments when we were alone with our baby were rare. It was as if we were inside a whirring machine with cogs constantly turning. There were all the conversations with hospital staff, texts and emails to answer, friends and family to see. JV was the sweet calm nucleus at the centre of it all. His heart was the tiny mitochondrion, an engine that valiantly kept pumping. I needed more time to tune in to him. To stroke his smooth cool cheeks, to watch the stillness of him as he slept. To simply be with him.

Day 8, Sunday

I chose a white gown with little blue boats embroidered just below the neckline for JV to wear to mass. The gown was in Sands' basket of gifts. I was grateful and wondered whose hands had made it. With it, JV would wear the white hand-knitted booties and hat that Amy had given him.

The plan was to stop for fifteen minutes at the kaikan en route to the cathedral. My mother and Roy thought this was too ambitious but I was determined, thinking of all the support I'd received from the Buddhist community. 'World peace chanting is just as important as mass,' I insisted.

By nine in the morning we were showered and polished and put together. My hair was brushed, earrings were in, lipstick was on. Roy had put on a shirt and aftershave. I felt as though we were going to the equivalent of a debutantes' ball, presenting our new family to the outside world for the first time.

Tisha arrived to drive us. 'Right,' she said, 'how's the little man? I'll just check his dressing before we go.' She unwound the bandage and lifted the padding while JV lay in my arms. 'There's some seepage. It looks like there's been some bleeding. Sorry, guys, we're going to have to change it.'

She called Dr W, who was on duty. Once again the rigmarole began. When we lay JV down in the bassinet he began crying straight away and cried through the whole dressing change. I didn't know if he was in pain, or now knew the routine of dressing changes and didn't like it. I swallowed down emotion, but a lump rose in my throat like a plum ready to burst.

'We're going to have to put him inside this,' Tisha said, holding up what looked like a black plastic bin liner, 'in case anything happens while we are out.' I realised in a split second that the bag would catch the spurting blood if JV's heart vessels burst.

'Fine,' I said, gritting my teeth. 'But let's put his purple sleeping bag over the top of the bag.' What new mother wants to present her new baby to the world for the first time in a black plastic bag? At the time I wasn't conscious of how worried Dr W was about JV. Roy told me later he had tears in his eyes as we left the hospital and I would read in his notes:

Dressing changed. Bloody ooze and pungent discharge from wound. Small clot adhered to underside of heart and at risk of bleeding. Family aware of this. Still OK to go to church. Tisha accompanying and has emergency bag suitable to manage massive bleed. Tisha will alert clergy of church to baby's condition ahead of time. Remains dusky but active on handling.

Dr W had also prepared a letter explaining why we had to hold JV in our arms in the car rather than putting him in a car seat, in case we were stopped by police.

> Should you find Jesus in the arms of his parents whilst in a motioning vehicle, [we ask] that his parents not be questioned and delayed on their journey, in view of the extenuating circumstances around this baby boy.
>
> Jesus is for terminal, palliative care. He was born at term on 26th October 2014 and not expected to survive the pregnancy or delivery. ...
>
> Our specialist providers are very encouraging of this family to continue to foster as much 'normality' as they can in anticipation of their son's passing. The Wellington Ambulance base have also been notified at the discharge of this infant for terminal care and are aware that, should contact be made with the team, he not be resuscitated.

Finally, we were in the car. We were running late. It was nine-thirty-five and mass started at ten. Roy and Mum tried to talk me out of stopping at the Buddhist centre but I dug my toes in. 'Even if it's just for a few minutes. It's important to me.' They sighed and agreed. Jimi and Camilla met us at the entrance. We sat at the back of the hall, which was thrumming with the sound of chanting. We were there only five minutes, but I was glad my baby got to experience the chanting he'd heard throughout my pregnancy.

At Sacred Heart Cathedral we found Father Lyons in the foyer with Brendon, Brendon's wife Isabelle, Maggie and Dad. It was just after ten; they had waited for us to arrive before beginning the mass.

We entered the church, which was brimming with people. Pews had been set aside for us at the front. 'Today is All Souls day,' Father Lyons began, 'a day for remembering those who have died. Yesterday was All Saints Day when we honoured the saints, and we have a little saint on his way to heaven amongst us today. You may have heard me talk about baptising a baby at dawn last Sunday. He wasn't even expected to live hours, and yet here he is, one week later, with us today. His parents made a brave decision to bring this baby into the world even though they knew his heart condition was fatal. His mother, Emma, tells me that every moment they have is precious. It is another moment to love him. Yet his life is very much held in the balance. If anything happens during the service the family may have to leave.'

I'd had no idea Father Lyons was going to tell our story. The upset of the morning receded. I felt the whole of the congregation was behind us, holding JV and us in their hearts. Because it was an important mass there was a full choir singing from the balcony. Choral singing had never sounded so angelic. I slipped into a reverie, imagining myself flying through pinkish clouds, my baby leading the way.

JV slept peacefully through the entire service. Afterwards we went into the side chapel where, to my surprise, we were greeted by about twenty friends. I'd had no idea they were coming and guessed Mum and Roy had invited them. We were hugged, JV was admired, we were told how brave we were, how moved people felt by our story.

A Polish woman introduced herself and told me with a certain urgency, 'You don't know me, but I have been praying for you throughout your pregnancy. I want you to know I heard a message during the service. Your baby's heart is outside his body because it's so full with love his body couldn't contain it.'

As we left, Brendon said, 'That mass today was the very reason the bricks were laid to build this cathedral. Some children don't get as much love in their whole life as you have given your son.'

The truth was I'd never felt as much love as I had since JV was born. I thought about an interview I'd heard in which American writer

Rebecca Solnit talked about the effects disasters can have on people. They can throw us into the present and give rise to a deep sense of connection with others, she said. You can feel as if you've been given a kind of spiritual awakening when you're close to mortality in a way that makes you feel more alive. This was what the days with JV were like. They were infused with a beautiful poignancy. Before returning to the hospital we stopped off at our house and ate lunch there. 'Hijito, this is your home,' Roy told JV.

The day before this, my stepfather Al had set off on a gruelling bike ride. The K2 is a race of 200 kilometres and Al had done two laps, 400 kilometres, beginning at night. He was riding in honour of JV and wore a heart on his shirt with our son's name on it. That evening he sent an email:

Well JV, my Ride for Heart is done. You'll have been at mass today. I was riding my bike instead of celebrating with you, but you have been in my heart all the time, believe me. Let me explain.

On this ride there are some difficulties. To start with, the night is dark, cold and unknown. Rolling along in your little pool of light, you feel very small with emptiness all about you, a little bit of road always ahead. Whangapoua is a long steep hill rising from sea level to a saddle high in the forest of the Coromandel ranges. The ride back down is twisty and fast, whipping the bike round bend after bend, wind tugging at your glasses. This hill is the biggest challenge ... My heart rate was 150–160 beats per minute, just like yours. And on those hills, some of the time, I breathed in every second. You do too, I've counted, so I know how hard that is, and what it feels like. ... You have such courage, JV, and in that dark I only had to think of you to keep going when I felt bad.

Seven hours later the sky lightens and birds sing all around you in the forest. I rode into the light, warmth returned, and I could see where I was and the journey ahead. … There's a bend in the coast far ahead. Go over this rise, under that tree, over that bridge, on and on. Next time you look at the bend it's much nearer, you can see trees on it. … Bit by bit your journey passes.

So, JV, if you find yourself alone in a cold dark night and it seems as if nobody is there, and there is nothing any more, just be your brave self and hold on a little while. Maybe you will hear birdsong, then see a lightening around you. You will find there is no more cold, and you [are] bathed in eternal light.

Amen.

I was crying by the time I finished reading this. For a long time Al's and my relationship had been difficult, but I felt the accumulated hurts and judgements being washed away by the love he was expressing for my son.

Day 9, Monday

'You're down the end of the hallway so hopefully it'll be nice and quiet for you,' Anna said. With her pale hair streaked with pink and her mauve T-shirt, the hospice nurse made me think of a fairy. 'We've made some signs you can put on the door too.'

The signs said 'Shhh… little prince sleeping' and 'Mum and Dad getting some rest'. On a noticeboard in the room the staff had pinned butterflies and bumblebees, the kind you might see in a nursery.

Earlier that day I'd sat in the olive-green La-Z-Boy with JV suckling on a bottle as the world we'd created in the Pōhutukawa Room was dismantled.

'Now, is there anything else you think you might need?' Anna asked.

'We need to store JV's milk in a fridge,' Roy said. 'Do you have a little one we could use?'

'We don't usually have them for the rooms but I'll see what I can do,' Anna said. A short time later she returned with a small fridge ordinarily used by staff in their room.

That evening, with Uncle Marty and Aunt Alayne, we toasted our new home and the first week of JV's life with strawberry champagne and party hats.

JV had seemed well that day. I was amazed that he had changed so much in the space of a week. His cheeks had become chubbier and he no longer had the freshly hatched look of a tiny newborn.

Hospice notes:

17:45 Emma and Roy are happy to be staying in a slightly less clinical environment with access to 'outside'. I have not examined JV except to look at his lovely face which was cyanosed as he was sleeping in his mother's arms. I have charted paracetamol for general pain and discomfort. I have also charted morphine for dyspnoea or pain/distress in case of any sudden event.

22:36 JV and his parents Emma and Roy have spent the afternoon settling into the unit. JV has been drinking EBM/formula on demand, tolerating well and winding/burping appropriately. Wet nappies, family are managing nappy changes. Sleeps best when being held by Emma and Roy. Aunt Phoebe is assisting by caring for JV overnight while they sleep.

Via my sister, we received another text from John Campbell:

Hello from Auckland where the latest news of JV's transcendent and miraculous life has filled us all with great pride. JV, you are remarkable.

And the fact that you don't even know how remarkable you are makes you all the more remarkable … every moment you stay is a moment more in which you remind us all that what matters most in life is how you make people feel. And you make people feel love. Which is the coolest thing there is, JV. … Your auntie Phoebe is part of our family, even though she's a terrible hippie and only eats plants. We're delighted she's staying with you. … Thanks for being, JV. Thanks for reminding us what really matters in life.

Day 10, Tuesday

'Would you like a cup of tea and cake? It's black forest gateau today.' The way the volunteer asked the question implied we'd be doing him a favour by accepting. After the cake I spent a blissful twenty minutes in a massage chair. I could hardly believe my luck. It was such a change from a hospital where the focus had been on diagnosis, treatment and monitoring. At the hospice the emphasis was on comfort and care. When the fridge from the staff room conked out they purchased us another one. At the end of the day Anna asked, 'Has anything not met your expectations today? Is there anything else we can do to support you guys?' If there was such a thing as a hospice fairy tale, this was it.

The notes reflected the intricate attention:

15:24 Very gentle chimes offered to JV's Dad and he accepted. I have left the chimes in JV's room and explained that if they choose to have gentle music then the chimes can be softly played.

16:25 Emma received a relaxation massage today in the interview room. Roy declined massage at this stage. Emma off for an afternoon nap. Grandma has taken up offer of counselling and will book time for the next few days.

We bathed JV in the afternoon. I was thankful for my mother's expertise. She showed me how to put my hand under his armpit so he didn't slide too far into the water. We had to be careful the dressings wrapped around his chest didn't get wet. Afterwards, swathed in a blanket patterned with red circus characters, his skin looked extra pink.

That night the vecinos brought us dinner. The vecinos – 'neighbours' – were the international gang of friends Roy used to live with before he moved in with me. Olga was from the Netherlands, Nacho from Argentina, Karen from Malaysia, and Nick was Chinese Canadian. We sat around a low table in the hospice's large lounge and ate fish pie, Malaysian rice, chickpea curry, guacamole and cake. The vecinos were like a portable party that had landed in the hospice.

Day 11, Wednesday

'Are there any alternatives to the current dressing changes?' I asked Dr W. I was worried about JV's comfort and the risk of infection.

It turned out he had been thinking about this. 'I have considered skin grafts, although that would mean a general anaesthetic, which poses great risks,' he said.

'Would the kind of shield I saw for baby Audrina be possible?' I said. Audrina was the ectopia cordis baby I'd seen on YouTube, who had been successfully operated on and wore a pink plastic shield to protect her heart in the months following surgery.

'The idea of a shield has merits, although bugs could get trapped beneath. And who would make it?' Although this was not promising I realised how hard Dr W was working for us. He confessed to having sleepless nights over the question of how best to care for JV.

I wanted to buy a cake and card for the midwives who had looked after us in the Pōhutukawa Room. My mother thought I'd be better off resting as the night shifts holding JV were still exhausting, but I wouldn't be swayed. Roy also had plans. He wanted to go to the Department of Internal Affairs to register JV's birth and get his birth certificate. We set off on our missions, leaving JV with my mother.

When I arrived at the supermarket I realised I was barely up to shopping. The choices seemed overwhelming. Eventually I picked a crimson-red velvet cake with white icing. Back at the hospital, a friend of my mother helped me decorate it with tiny pebbles and jelly snakes that spelled out: 'JV – 10 days old – Joy.' I wrote in the card on JV's behalf:

Dear Dr W, Dr D, Tisha and all the smiling midwives and neonatal team, Thank you for caring, loving and believing in me during my time in the Pōhutukawa Room. After one week my dad said the room wasn't big enough for all our love, so we've moved to a bigger place where a tūī comes to visit me in a tree outside the window. Dad says this new place still might not be big enough for all our love and wants to go home. Mum says we'll see how it goes. Your kindness and sensitivity make a huge different in family lives (but you probably already know that). Your skill and knowledge are a taonga. X Jesús Valentino (10 days old!)

Day 12, Thursday

Welts appeared like red islands on JV's pale neck. 'It could be a hormone rash, or one caused by milk spilling on to his neck,' the hospice doctor said when she saw him that morning.

'Do other babies get rashes like these?' I asked.

'Oh yes, my daughter did. Use a barrier cream to protect his skin and it should clear up.' I was relieved to hear this was a regular baby complaint.

That afternoon we went out for a walk. We'd gone only a few blocks when JV began crying fractiously in a way that wasn't like him. Back at the hospice we discovered he needed a nappy change, and after a feed he drifted back to sleep. Perhaps his distress was normal? Or was it a sign his heart was deteriorating? It was impossible to know.

Hospice notes:

22:13 Baby JV was seen by Dr S, prescribed some Tui balm for red blotchy patches under chin and neck. JV seems to be settled and quiet tonight, have not seen any family pacing the floor with him. Family all seem relaxed and loving, caring beautifully for little JV.

My father came to do the first part of the night shift. In the early hours of the morning I sent another email update:

7/11/14, 3:17am

Queridos amigos y familia,

Here I am burning the midnight oil again with JV asleep in my arms. He will be two weeks old on Sunday & it might be time to review our sleeping policy that he never gets put down!

On Monday we moved from the hospital to Mary Potter Hospice, which was a great move. We have a lovely light room with French doors that look out to a patio with trees. The staff here are exceptionally nice.

Against all expectations JV continues to thrive. This week he had a gummy eye & a rash yesterday, but these are regular baby complaints. We toasted his first week with bubbly & took a cake over to the hospital staff on Wednesday to celebrate his 10 days.

Thanks for your continued love & kindness.

Emma & Roy

Day 13, Friday

My email saying the baby was thriving proved false. By the morning JV's rash had got worse and his whole body was now covered with inflamed red blotches.

'It's probably related to circulation problems that indicate his heart is not coping so well now,' Dr W told us when he came to visit.

'Will the rash be causing him discomfort?' I asked.

'Adult heart patients who have this symptom say it feels like a burning under the skin as the blood that is pooling can't be shifted.'

This news killed me. My poor wee darling. Was the tide turning now? Was this the end of the golden weather in our son's life?

Dr W recommended we give him paracetamol every four hours, supplemented with morphine if he still seemed in distress.

Until now I had been reluctant to use Panadol, cautious about unnecessarily drugging my baby, but now I wanted to give him whatever he needed, as much as he needed – anything to stop his pain. The Panadol calmed him, but it also made him sleepy. He was like a floppy rag doll in our arms.

1430 Dr W talked to family re change in Jesus, heart getting tired, circulation failing, not feeding as well, appears more grumpy. Plan: start 4 hourly pamol (1ml)

In the afternoon Roy and I walked with JV to the end of the street, where a sloping grass lawn marked the beginning of the Mt Victoria town belt. It was a lovely warm day and the three of us sat peacefully in the sun. In that moment I told myself the key was to stay in the present, to enjoy what could be enjoyed. More important than the destination was the journey JV was taking us on. After the initial wonderment that our son was so well at birth we'd been lulled into feeling his being alive was normal, yet a part of me knew we were living in a bubble that couldn't last. In my mind I saw the ornate mandalas of coloured sands created by Buddhist monks that are erased in a matter of minutes.

That evening Father Lyons came, bearing a red rose for JV from the archbishop's garden. We had a sweet quiet conversation. He reminded me that during the pregnancy I'd said we wanted to love our baby for as long as he lived, that continuing the pregnancy would mean more opportunities for love, and that doors would be opened I couldn't yet imagine. 'Your intuition proved to be correct,' he said.

Hospice notes:

22:27 Roy and Emma are able to articulate that they see signs that JV will not be with them for much longer. They note that he appears more sleepy – they attribute this to Pamol but pleased he is comfortable. Sucking well from bottle when hungry. Parents have taken JV out for a walk this afternoon and enjoyed being outside. Family will ring if they need support overnight, still prefer whispers when speaking in the room.

Day 14, Saturday

On the hill above the convent, purple lupins cascaded down in a burst of wild spring growth. Viewed from a distance, the patch of lupins made the shape of an enormous heart. We were visiting the Home of Compassion founded by Mother Suzanne Aubert, the nun in whose name Father Lyons had asked for a miracle for our baby. Roy had had the idea of visiting Mother Aubert's grave with JV. Tisha had generously given up her Saturday to accompany us. Tisha knew the convent well: raised a Catholic, she had visited it as a child.

I sat on a chair beside Suzanne Aubert's small black headstone, feeding JV from a bottle. Silently I prayed, 'God, if it's your will and my baby's will that by some miracle he stays with us, may his heart be fixed. If not, may he pass peacefully.' Afterwards we explored the convent grounds, which used to include an orphanage. Built into a large slab of rock was a grotto to Our Lady of Lourdes. Around the corner, hidden behind old buildings, was a garden. It was the epitome of fecund. Flowers bloomed, bumblebees hummed, birds chirped, butterflies fluttered, spinach, rhubarb and beans raced skyward. A rabbit hopped into bushes.

'This must be the best place to be in all of Wellington right now,' Roy said. We stayed for hours, sprawled out on the grass, enjoying the warmth on our skin, the sweet smells. The sun and fresh air seemed to do JV a world of good. The rash on his skin vanished.

That night, though, he was again fractious and unsettled. Around five in the morning he was inconsolable. Both Roy and I wanted to believe this was normal baby behaviour, rather than his heart failing, and yet the idea he was in pain and we weren't giving him relief was unbearable. Eventually we called for the nurse, who gave him morphine via a syringe. He immediately slept.

I couldn't rest afterwards, even though I was very tired. Questions circled in my head. Was our desire to stop his cries about soothing ourselves or him?

18:03 JV is more blue and sleepy. Longer periods of being unsettled, less able to suck and spitting majority of milk from his mouth. Strategy for the afternoon is to give half doses of pamol every 2 hrs. Have given Roy the laptop to make it easier for him to contact family in Peru.

01:25 Roy came and requested JV be given his pamol at 0045hrs as he was awake. As it is charted 6hrly I phoned Dr E for his approval to give this early. Roy was concerned when I gave him the pamol that I had given him the incorrect amount. He thought he should be having 1ml, not 2mls as I had drawn up. I discussed with Roy that there are different strengths of pamol and that previous staff must have been administering the stronger strength in order for a smaller volume to be given. Roy has needed reassurance about this – may need further clarifying in the morning.

Day 15, Sunday

That morning I accidentally gave JV too much paracetamol and he was too sleepy to feed afterwards. Later, two NICU staff we didn't know came to change his dressings. He was distraught, and I was distraught at all we were inflicting on him. The bandages, the syringes of paracetamol, and now morphine squirted into his mouth. I was keenly aware of his fragility. What was keeping him alive?

That afternoon we had another outing with Tisha – this time to the native bird sanctuary, Zealandia. We walked to where feeding stations were set up for kākā, the brown native parrots with russet red under their wings. I lay on my back in the grass while a dozen kākā wheeled in circles above us.

As we walked back to the entrance a small group had gathered to admire a baby tuatara, the endemic New Zealand reptile. Roy, who had

JV in his sling, stopped to chat with them.

'What's his name?' one of the women asked.

'Jesús Valentino.'

'Oh, that's a sweet name. Funnily we heard about a baby called Valentino at mass this morning.'

'Yes,' said another woman. 'There's a little Valentino born with his heart outside his chest, who is alive against all expectations.'

'Were you at Sacred Heart Cathedral?'

'Yes. How did you know?'

'This was this baby Father Lyons was talking about,' Roy said.

Hospice notes:

15:48 JV has just returned from outing. Have caught up with Emma and Andrea. Family continue to give half doses of paracetamol (25mg) but should be giving 1ml at a time … NICU nurse Tisha has reiterated this as JV is more settled with the full paracetamol dose; if ineffective can safely have morphine as well. Some of this info may need to be repeated as parents are getting tired.

22:28 JV has been quite unsettled this shift, difficult to pacify, crying more and not sleeping more than 30 minutes. Given pamol 50mg at 1600, required morphine at 20:05. Drinking small volumes. Emma worried about potential dehydration. Discussed it may be that JV is finding the demand on his heart too much, reducing his appetite.

Day 16, Monday

'¡Hijito, sabes que? Te queremos mucho, mucho, mucho.' Roy was cradling our sleeping boy in a pale yellow blanket. We had just Skyped

Roy's parents in Peru. It was another sunny day in a spring that had been unusually full of sunny days.

'Yes, darling, we love you so so so so much.'

I meant those words with every ounce of my being. I'd thought my little boy might not make it through the night but here he was, with us still.

My sister Phoebe had flown back down from Auckland the day before and offered to do the first part of the night shift, but JV wouldn't settle. He winced and coughed and squirmed. He waved his left arm as if fighting something.

When I took over at midnight he calmed down. I felt glad I could soothe him but knew I couldn't hold him through the whole night: my body couldn't survive on the sparse amount of sleep I'd had in the past two weeks.

At two a.m. JV was distressed again. I rang the bell and asked for more morphine after his paracetamol. At first the nurse said no: according to the notes he was supposed to have morphine six-hourly and he'd had some at ten o'clock. Finally, however, she brought it. Roy took over and I drifted into a heavy slumber.

I woke at seven in the morning, feeling much better. JV slept on. He was due for another paracetamol dose at eight-thirty: Tisha had impressed on us the importance of giving this at six-hourly intervals to stave off discomfort before it came. I didn't want to wake JV but, in the end, gave it to him by syringe at nine-thirty. He roused but didn't want to feed. He couldn't seem to swallow. An hour later I saw that the paracetamol I'd given him was still sitting in a glob in the side of his cheek.

We were now in the hardest phase. I wished we had more video footage of him. I wished I had spent more time simply being in his company.

Baby deteriorated overnight, not very responsive or alert. Nil feeds tolerated, spilling saliva and pamol.

2 hrly Panadol suppositories, can have 2 hrly morphine. Serious change in Jesus' condition in past 24 hours.

'I had a text from Jimi this morning. He is in Japan and was chanting with all his might for JV at the very moment President Ikeda unexpectedly drove past.' Camilla, who had come to visit, was passing on this news. It was auspicious. Daisaku Ikeda was the highly respected leader of the SGI. I was grateful that even in Japan JV was being remembered.

Camilla and Phoebe knelt beside the bed and chanted while I sat in the La-Z-Boy and chanted above JV as softly as I could. I didn't think he would want to be bombarded with full-voiced chanting. He was sleeping again, and his breathing was so slight, so slow. It had been more than twelve hours since he'd eaten or swallowed anything.

Before she left, Camilla had a message for me from a women's leader in Japan. 'She said you should chant fiercely for JV to live for another day.' I knew this message was meant to impart hope, but I couldn't help thinking, what if my baby doesn't want to live another day? Who would we be keeping him alive for?

In the afternoon, we had one of the rare times when Roy, JV and I were alone together. Roy and I lay down in bed, nestling JV between us. When he woke up crying we called the nurse, who gave him more Panadol and morphine. Roy and I sat on the edge of the bed together. I held my son in my arms the way he liked. 'We're so proud of you and so happy you have stayed with us so long,' I told him. 'But it's okay to go. I promise we'll be strong.'

JV's breathing got slower and slower. I don't know the moment he died. It was imperceptible. We sat with him for about ten minutes and then we rang the bell. Dr Ensor, the head of the hospice, came. He seemed to know JV was dead just by looking at him. 'He died beautifully,' he said, tears in his eyes. 'He chose wonderful parents.'

Strange as it sounds, I felt touched by a kind of incandescent peace. It was not unlike the feeling I'd had when we decided to continue the pregnancy. It was as if an angel was encasing me in its soft silver wings.

After

Hospice notes:

> Cause of Death: Cardia Ectopia and complex congenital heart disease
> Summary: […] With assiduous input from the paediatric team who came
> across each day, doing the dressings and supporting the family, JV deteriorated
> uneventfully, using paracetamol for comfort and then some morphine over
> the last few days. The family were able to get out for visits during the day,
> again with the support of the paediatric team. JV died very peacefully on
> Monday afternoon 1545, held by his mother.

My mother and sister returned from a walk and Tisha came from the
hospital. Together we sponged JV's body, changed the dressing around
his heart, and dressed him in fresh clothes. Then I sat with him in my
arms and the women began to pack our things, like a vacuum cleaner
hoovering up evidence of our presence.

'We haven't done JV's hand- and footprints,' I said. There was a kit
in the Pōhutukawa Room. Had we missed the opportunity? Did the
imprint of a hand or foot change when a body was no longer alive?

'I'll go back to the hospital and get the kit,' Tisha said. When she
returned she made prints of JV's hands and feet. The prints were silver
ink on white paper, fine lines that spiralled like a miniature labyrinth
and would only ever belong to our son.

Javier came with his SUV to transport our things home. Once we
were in the car with JV in the basket beside me on the back seat, I got
out again to return to our room. I wanted to open the French doors, to
release anything that needed to be set free or follow us home.

Much of the rest of that night is a blank. I remember that we moved a table into the lounge and placed JV on it in his basket. Javier stayed for dinner. Dad and Maggie visited. We moved JV's basket into our bedroom to be with us for the night.

I kept expecting my baby's eyes to open, for him to stir as I laid my hand on his head or adjusted his blanket. I was accustomed to seeing him asleep. Was this any different? Surely he would soon need to be fed and cry to be picked up.

Next day we moved JV back into the lounge. Around him in his basket I placed a rose quartz crystal, his knitted panther, a small statue of Jesus, the red rose from the archbishop's garden. Around the basket I lit candles. At the head I placed our statue of Guadalupe and a white orchid plant. The stem of white flowers bowed in salute above our baby.

First thing that morning I'd taken JV out of the basket and cradled him in my arms. I didn't want him to be left alone. Roy had waited in our bedroom with him while I had a shower. I had stayed with him while Roy made breakfast. I bumbled my way through, wishing I came from a culture where the rules governing how you looked after a body were clear and tried and true. I wanted to be sure we were doing it right, treating our baby with utmost respect.

Later that day I took JV out of his basket again and unwrapped his blankets. His stomach had changed colour and was now a motley blue and purple. He was cold and his limbs were becoming rigid. Since he wouldn't be embalmed, we'd placed the cooling pad underneath his mattress. It was blue nylon and attached to what looked like a fan heater. This gadget made a whirring noise. I didn't like the look or sound of it. The candles I'd placed around the basket had to be blown out in case the nylon caught alight.

* * *

'Do you think there could be Buddhist chanting at the funeral?' Roy's question to Father Lyons took me by surprise. I wanted to ask Camilla to speak, but I hadn't imagined actual chanting.

Father Lyons seemed to quite like the idea. 'Instead of a full Catholic mass, we could make it a service of thanksgiving and celebration so all who are present feel welcome, whether they are Catholic or not,' he said. I thought this suggestion very gracious on his part.

The funeral planning had begun. The service would be held in four days, on Friday at eleven a.m. The funeral director, Fiona, arrived. She was efficiently taking notes and had a great many ideas. 'What about flowers?' she asked. 'I thought you might like Peruvian lilies alongside a New Zealand flower, to represent JV's dual roots? And how about a keepsake for all those who came to the funeral to remember JV – a little toy, or perhaps a decoration to hang on the Christmas tree?' I'd thought of asking friends to bring flowers from their gardens but the thought of organising a keepsake for the seventy-five people we estimated would attend made me quake inside.

The list of things to do to seemed overwhelming. Fiona talked rapidly and her many questions made my head spin. Would JV be in a coffin, or would we carry him in the basket he was lying in now? If a coffin, would it be open or closed? I didn't really want a closed coffin, but I wondered if the sight of a dead baby would be too much for some people. If we used the coffin Vicki and her husband had made, would we like to attach a cross to the lid? Would there be songs? Yes. Live or recorded? I didn't know.

Would there be a cup of tea after the service? This seemed natural to me but Roy had other ideas. 'In Peru you don't eat or drink until the burial is over, so we should meet somewhere later,' he said.

'But not everyone will come to the burial,' I said. 'At least if we have a cup of tea after the service we could say hello to people.'

'Well, let's have a cup of tea before the funeral service.'

This proposal seemed utterly mad.

And there was something else: we were talking about a burial but we hadn't confirmed we wanted this. Roy and I turned out to have different views on this as well. Bodies are not cremated in Peru, and he found the concept foreign and somewhat violent. For me, leaving our baby underground in a strange place, surrounded by people he didn't know, was more disturbing. What if he was cold and lonely? If we had his ashes at home, he would still be close to us. I imagined myself hugging an urn to my chest for comfort.

That afternoon, Roy and I were still debating. It was five to four and the death notice had to be sent to the paper by four. Roy had told me I should write the notice, and I had come up with:

Jesús Valentino (b. 26/10/14), beloved son of Emma Gilkison and Roy Costilla, passed peacefully in his parents' arms on Monday afternoon. We will always love you JV. 'Plant naught in the garden of thy heart but the rose of love.' A service of thanksgiving and celebration will be held at 11am on Friday at Sacred Heart Cathedral.

Roy wanted to add the sentence: *JV, you gave us faith, courage and the peace of God.* My issue was with 'peace of God'. What about the peace of Buddhism? Would people think I had made a whole-scale conversion to Catholicism?

'Emma, you have written the whole thing. All I am asking for is one sentence,' Roy protested.

I relented. I was too fragile for arguing, and I realised the irony of my getting wound up about being seen as more Christian than I was when my son was called Jesús Valentino.

'Unfortunately, you can't bury JV at the Home of Compassion without a law change because it's not a sanctioned place for public burial. A special law was passed for Suzanne Aubert to be buried there. But if you choose to have JV cremated the nuns say his ashes can be kept in the chapel.'

The hospital chaplain Father Patrick had come to visit and this was the latest development in our discussion about burial vs. cremation. Father Lyons had thought perhaps JV could be buried next to Suzanne Aubert and Father Patrick had spoken to the nuns on our behalf.

Roy liked the idea of JV's resting place being the Home of Compassion but didn't want a cremation. I wanted a cremation but didn't think I wanted to leave his ashes at the Home of Compassion.

'The other thing the nuns said is that they have a section of plots at Karori Cemetery, and they would be willing to gift one of these to you if you wanted JV to be buried there.'

The options were making me giddy. Next day, with Phoebe, we set out to visit cemeteries and crematoriums, hoping to find consensus. In the office of Karori Cemetery an administrator marked on a map where to find the plots belonging to the Home of Compassion nuns. There was also a section of the cemetery where only infants were buried, and she marked this too. First, we went to the cemetery's chapel, which doubled as a crematorium. Light shone through rainbow-coloured stained-glass windows and reflected on the brass plaques that lined the walls, inscribed with the names of deceased.

'Mostly families don't want to witness the cremation.' Tim, a lanky grounds worker in a fluoro vest, was giving us a tour of the crematorium. I felt differently. If JV was going to be cremated, I wanted to be with him until the final moment. I needed to know exactly what was going to happen to my baby and how.

Tim showed us the conveyor belt that carried a coffin through maroon curtains from the chapel into a room behind it. In contrast with the richly decorated chapel, the small room had bare concrete walls painted white. A bench with rollers fed coffins through a door into a furnace.

'Intense heat is created inside by burning fuel. Usually the coffin and body are incinerated by a column of flames,' Tim explained in his thick northern England accent, 'but it's a bit different for babies. Because they are much lighter, if we were to feed their coffins through this door, the heat from inside the furnace could throw the coffin right back out.'

'So what do you do?' I asked.

Tim took us through another door, and we walked single file along a hot grimy narrow passageway leading to the back of the furnace. He pointed at a small hatch at floor level where our baby's coffin would be inserted. This was not a place where we could gather to be with JV while he was cremated. On an abstract level, I didn't believe the deceased had any use for the weight of the flesh: the soul flies free. But examining the cremation process this closely it felt hot, mechanical and brutal. Perhaps it was not what I wanted for JV after all.

The Home of Compassion's graves were under a line of pine trees on a sloping bank at the eastern side of the cemetery. I liked the idea of my baby resting with the nuns, who could keep an eye on him, but the area was shady and I couldn't see myself going there to while away an afternoon.

The infants' section of the cemetery was on higher ground, with a warmer, sunnier aspect. The small graves were lovely, adorned with windmills, teddies, statues of cherubs and even Tinkerbell from *Peter Pan*. They were the most colourful in the cemetery and you could feel the tenderness and love surrounding them. Seeing these graves was strangely comforting. They placed JV's story within a bigger story.

We had one more possibility to consider: a natural burial, where instead of having a deep grave and formal headstone a person is buried under a tree. I knew almost before we got there it was going to be a no. The cemetery at Makara was in a dramatic landscape near a fierce ocean – striking and impressive, but too wild and windswept a place to leave my baby. Perhaps the infants' section of Karori Cemetery was the best place for JV. I'd realised standing there I would not be afraid to bury my son. He would not be lonely in that sweet place. I imagined him making friends with the other babies.

We were flooded with cards and flowers. Many people had written at length, more than the standard few lines. Despite all the beautiful words I was inwardly in turmoil. When JV was alive it had been easy just to look at him and feel good. Now I struggled to cope with each new wave of visitors, with the many conversations, with the details of the funeral. I was like a cracked eggshell on the verge of disintegrating.

The day before the funeral I still hadn't had a chance to compose my tribute. Early in the afternoon I sat down next to my baby to write it, my heart aching. At five o'clock Dad, Maggie and other friends and family arrived. I was vaguely aware Roy had made a plan to recite a rosary for JV. I retreated into our bedroom and asked Roy to let me know when it was going to begin. I began trying on clothes to wear to the funeral but nothing looked right.

Twenty minutes later I ventured out and found the rosary in full swing. Why hadn't anyone called me? Our lounge was full of people, some of whom I hardly knew. Roy had Skyped in his parents from Peru. The sounds of 'Hail Mary' rang out.

At first I thought there was nowhere for me to sit, but then I saw the seat next to JV's basket was empty. Why was no one sitting next to him? I felt violated, as if my lounge, my baby's sacred space, had been trampled on. When the rosary was finished, I said icily, 'It would be nice to be invited next time. Can I have a moment with JV please?'

A few of the South American women didn't seem to hear my request and stayed in the room. I wanted them out. I was beside myself. Luckily Amy arrived at that moment and rescued me. In my room I choked out hoarse sobs. She suggested a walk and we slipped out the back door. It was a mild early-summer evening and although I wasn't cold I was shivering. This meltdown was the product of too many people, too much pressure, too many texts, too many bunches of flowers, too much everything.

Slowly I began to feel calm and a bit less crazy. When we arrived home, most of the visitors had left. I went back to my bedroom to work on the photomontage for the service. Luke, Phoebe's partner, had assembled on his laptop photos taken by many people. This had seemed like a good idea but there were a staggering one and a half thousand. How on earth was I supposed to go through them all? What's more Luke's laptop was an Apple and I was used to PCs.

Then there was the question around how many photos were needed. This depended on the speed the photos would rotate and the length of the song that would play when the photos were up on the screen. These calculations felt far beyond what I was currently capable of. I decided to forgo the whole archive and limit my choice to photos I'd taken, which I could access on my laptop.

On the morning of JV's funeral I woke up confused, and still cross about what'd happened with the rosary. The house was filled with smoke. Roy was burning palo santo, a fragrant, incense-like wood from Peru believed to have healing powers. I snapped at him to open windows and doors. Shortly afterwards I went into the kitchen to get a glass of water.

A chaffinch was stuck behind a vase on the windowsill, trying to fly out. I shrieked and Roy appeared. He calmly took the vase off the windowsill. With a ruffle of his feathers, the chaffinch hopped on to the top of the stove, found a few grains of rice from the previous night's pilau and pecked a few. He then hopped on to the floor just a few feet away from us and cocked his head quizzically to one side. A minute later he exited through the back door as though he'd known how to leave all along.

There seemed something special about this incident. The bird appeared to be saying that if you were in a frightening situation, there was no need to fight against it. Don't struggle. You'll find the door you need to go through. This seemed to me how JV had lived his life, utterly trusting and accepting. With this thought I found the equanimity I was craving.

With Mum and Amy's help I undressed JV and took off his bandages. His crimson heart was like a rose in full bloom on his chest. It looked beautiful. I rubbed scented oil over him, the same oil I'd rubbed over my belly during pregnancy. I cut some locks of his silky brown hair and dressed him in a white gown. Amy helped put a little foundation and powder on his face. I gazed at my darling. It was my last time to see his naked body, to stroke his bare skin. After all the madness of the last few days what I needed most was to connect with my child.

Amy helped to get me dressed, put on my makeup, advised how the pink shawl I was wearing over my black dress should be draped, cleaned my shoes. Finally, we were ready. Roy and I carried the basket, threaded with fresh flowers, down the steps to the silver Mercedes we had been lent, and drove slowly around the bays. We arrived at the church fifteen minutes late, but it didn't matter. Father Lyons met us outside. 'Usually,' he said, smiling, 'it's the brides who keep me waiting.'

The church was filled with more than a hundred people, many more than I'd imagined would come. Together, Roy and I carried JV in his basket down the aisle to the accompaniment of the lullaby we'd often played him: 'A million tomorrows can all melt away, ere we forget all the love that we had today.'

Tina, a friend of my mother's, read out my tribute:

My darling, I thought I was head over heels in love with you even before you were born, but nothing could prepare me for the joy of seeing your face and gazing into your beautiful eyes. How can I thank you enough for staying on earth long enough for us to become properly acquainted? … I'd be lying if I said I didn't miss you terribly but I promise I'll do my best to keep my heart open and not get lost in the pain. I will keep loving you forever. I will always be your mother and you will always be my son. Our connection will remain forever.

Then Roy spoke.

JV, you made me a father, you made us a family. JV, you bought us the peace of God.

My father had written a tribute in Māori. Afterwards, two of his friends stood up and sang a waiata. My mother addressed JV directly, telling him how proud she was of him, what a beautiful grandson he was, that he had given her the best days of her life. Camilla spoke of the power of the human heart to draw forth hope and courage, and help us rise above adversity, even in the midst of the greatest suffering. 'As we all know, the life of Jesús Valentino encapsulates the power of the heart,' she said. The massive gong she had brought from the kaikan rang out as she led us in chanting 'Nam-myoho-renge-kyo' three times. Roy's parents had sent a message from Lima and Roy asked Javier, who was filming the funeral, to read it out. Father Lyons asked my stepmother Maggie to read a homily.

At the end of the speeches, photos of JV appeared on the screen. Suddenly a soprano began to sing 'Ave Maria' from the church eves. Roy had asked for this exquisite song but I had no idea there would be a live performance, presumably organised by Father Lyons.

'You are now invited to place a flower in JV's basket,' Father Lyons told the people gathered. My sisters Eleanor, Meghan and Francie held wicker baskets filled with flowers picked from the gardens of our friends and family. After he'd placed his flower my Uncle Marty hugged us. After this there was a waterfall of hugs. I felt buoyed, lifted, afloat on something radiant.

My grandfather materialised. I was stunned. He and my late grand-mother had divorced on bad terms and he had remarried and fallen out of my life. I hadn't seen him in a decade. Now here he was. He'd recently had surgery and would soon be catching a bus back to Palmerston North, two hours away.

When the service was over, in the chapel on the side of the church Roy and I lifted JV from his basket into the coffin made by Vicki and her husband. Around him I placed a candle, an angel soap, a Jesus statue, a knitted teddy. I tucked him in with the poncho his grandparents had sent from Peru. I hoped these talismans would give my son strength in the realm he was travelling to.

My father, Maggie and my sisters had organised food and drink in the hall next door. After greeting funeral-goers there, Roy and I, with family and close friends, made our way to the cemetery. Father Lyons had a plane to catch so Roy had found another priest to conduct the burial rites. By chance Father Gerard had lived in Peru; as he led the prayers in Spanish a rainbow-coloured rosella flew overhead. As JV's coffin was lowered into the ground I stayed very still, kneeling on the grass, watching closely. Flowers were placed in the grave. Dirt was shovelled over. I needed to see every bit, to know it was real.

What I thought might be one of the hardest days of my life turned out to be one of the most special. The moments I'd feared – carrying the coffin in the church, seeing my son buried in the ground – were when I felt most of all the great love I had for him. To love him was to accept his journey. I knew when we buried him he was no longer in his body. No trace of his spirit remained within. It was okay to place him under the earth. This was not a dream. JV would not turn and wake up.

Two days later, a Sunday morning, Roy and I were sitting in the garden quietly singing '¿Cómo estás, Jesús Valentino?' when the chaffinch that had come into the kitchen on the morning of the funeral landed close to our feet. The chestnut-coloured feathers on his breast were well-preened and the brick-red feathers on his face gave his cheeks a rosy glow.

He hopped into the kitchen. I followed him. He flew down the hall to the bedroom that had JV's things from the hospital and hovered above them. I didn't want to frighten him. I closed the doors to the other rooms off the hallway and backed out into the garden. A minute later he hopped out the kitchen door and flew away, as if he knew exactly what he was doing all along.

That afternoon Roy and I walked hand-in-hand on a beach and watched kids practising lifesaving drills. After all we'd been through, I felt closer to him than ever. In the evening we went to a mass led by Father Patrick. To our surprise our real estate agent was in the congregation.

We needed to give her an answer in the next few days about whether we would buy Ariki Road.

Spontaneously we asked Father Patrick to dinner. A friend of Roy's had offered to cook. As we drank beer and ate, I decided if this was grief it was not so bad. There was so much joy still in thinking of our son.

Of course, it was never going to be that easy. The next week I began to find out what grief was really like. For several nights in a row I dreamed JV was in bed with us. The first night he needed cake and water – cake to feed the chaffinch, which still visited our garden every day, holy water to bless our house. In another dream I wondered if he should be buried naked. In another he lay in his coffin at the foot of our bed.

The questions in my dreams extended into my waking moments. How should I best care for JV now? Should I display more photos? Light a candle every evening? Sing to him? Offer him prayers or flowers? A part of me ached to know what my baby still needed from me. The thought that he might be okay, that he might not need anything, was strange.

'I'm worried I'm not doing enough to honour JV's spirit,' I confessed to Trish, who had come to visit, bearing coffee and muffins. 'Never think that, when you've given JV so much love,' she said. 'You've already honoured him beautifully in life and death.'

'When did you give birth?' the squat midwife asked. She sounded impatient.

'26th of October.'

'And where is baby? At home?'

I was at an appointment at the women's clinic of the hospital. I'd been having difficulty going to the toilet since JV was born: it felt as though my back passage had been stretched into a new unfamiliar shape during labour. I'd waited for over an hour to be seen. I'd assumed the midwife would have read my notes.

I couldn't contain my sobs. 'My baby died,' I sputtered out.

The midwife, trying to comfort me, started asking questions about what had happened but I didn't want her comfort or to share JV's story with her. I just wanted to be treated. Finally, the doctor, a young registrar, arrived. He examined me and declared everything looked normal. I should drink more kiwifruit juice, do more pelvic floor exercises. And that was that.

That week I had many lists in my head of things I thought I needed to do. Sort out the chaos in the spare room. Buy gifts to thank people who'd helped us. Reply to emails. Sort out bills. Hand-wash the cream heirloom shawl JV had been wrapped in so often. Clean his bottles, which sat on the bench, still filmed with milk. Sort out the fridge and the cupboards, which were overflowing with food we'd been given.

I ordered postcards, printed with an image of Roy, JV and me, for thank-you notes. I also wanted about a hundred photos printed. On my first foray into town it was challenging to know where to park, how to interact with sales assistants. Walking into a store to look for gifts almost undid me. I felt confused and nauseous.

Also on the list was the decision about Ariki Road. Were we going to buy the house at the reduced price? I could hardly fathom this. JV had been my raison d'être for months. Who was I now? If I didn't know that, how could I possibly know if I wanted to buy this house?

Mid-week, when I sat down before my altar to chant, I cracked up. I barely had the energy to force the words from my mouth. I cried dry hoarse sobs. Roy came and held me. I realised then I needed to stop. I had been in constant motion since going into labour nearly four weeks before. And now some part of me was screaming to be still. I sat on the couch and didn't move for the rest of the day. This felt entirely right.

'There is a little container with incense granules and people take three pinches from it, representing past, present and future, and place these on a lit charcoal.' Camilla was explaining the incense-offering ceremony held by SGI when someone dies. We were holding one for JV that night. It was going to be a low-key, intimate affair with people who knew us well. Dr W had called to apologise he hadn't been able to come to JV's funeral because of an urgent situation at work. When I told him about the incense-offering ceremony, he said he would like to come. There was a lovely symmetry to seeing him at the kaikan: our relationship with him had been a journey from mistrust to deep trust and appreciation.

Beside the altar there was a table with fresh flowers, two photos of JV, and the burning incense. While we chanted 'Nam-myoho-renge-kyo' people got up one by one to offer incense to JV. As I chanted I imagined my connection with JV as like fine shiny ribbons tethering us together. When I offered the three pinches of incense, my prayer for him was simple: I love you, I loved you and I will always love you.

After the chanting Camilla told a parable written by Nichiren in 1280. King Rinda had great strength and vigour and a happy kingdom as long as he heard the neighing of white horses. The white horses neighed only when they caught sight of white swans. One day the white swans disappeared, the horses stopped neighing, and the king's strength drained away. His kingdom fell into disarray. Eventually a disciple of the Buddha, Bodhisattva Ashvaghosha, called the swans back. The horses recommenced neighing and all was well in the kingdom again.

'The neighing horse,' Camilla said, 'is like the sound of chanting Nam-myoho-renge-kyo and we all have the power to be like Bodhisattva Ashvaghosha, a catalyst for our own well-being. Emma was a catalyst in her own life and the life of JV by the way she summoned love, compassion and wisdom.'

I got up to speak. Despite feeling so lost earlier in the week, I found myself standing confidently and making jokes. 'Next time we will call our baby Buddha,' I said.

'Why did JV live so much longer than you thought?' I asked Dr W the day after the ceremony. We had an appointment with him and Tisha to 'debrief'.

He told me again about the duct that JV used to help the transfer of oxygen around his body; this usually functioned only in utero. 'But I don't believe JV would have lived as long as he did if he hadn't had the care he got from you. Your love is at least half the reason he did so well,' she said. To hear this astute and rational doctor recognise the power of love was gratifying.

Both Dr W and Tisha had folders of notes. The handwriting of dozens of people was scrawled across pages and pages. It struck me how many people were part of the hospital machine that had looked after JV. Unbeknownst to us, we had been the subject of many conversations outside the Pōhutukawa Room.

I hadn't realised JV was the first baby to be admitted to the hospice. Dr W explained he had needed to get permission from the head of palliative care at Wellington Hospital to broker the agreement, and the hospice staff had had to be consulted to ensure they felt comfortable having a baby in their care.

* * *

In our letterbox I found a letter from the Earthquake Commission addressed to the owner of the house. I guiltily opened it and read details of a claim that had been made for cracks in the walls of 6 Ariki Road. We'd heard nothing of this and the discovery sent me into a spin. I spoke to the real estate agent. She said the cracks had been minor and the claim unimportant. She added, 'Don't be afraid to tell me now if you don't want to buy the house.'

I didn't know what I wanted. I was full of anxieties about the house purchase and didn't know whether they were justified. Roy, on the other hand, was clear that we should buy the house. By the end of the week I'd signed a purchase agreement, conditional on receiving the compliance tick from the city council that work on the foundations had been completed to an acceptable standard. I had no idea if this was the right thing to do.

It strikes me now as terrible timing to have been buying a house the week after our son had died.

That week I began throwing out dead flowers, which were beginning to spread their over-sweet smell through the house. There were many vases and it was a big job. Which flowers to keep, which to bin, how to consolidate? This seemingly simple task made me reel. I didn't know how to get on top of things. I felt physically and mentally weak, as if I had a bad case of flu. In a few days we were going to have a holiday in the Coromandel. I hoped the sea and the change of scene would help me recalibrate.

As we drove to Cooks Beach Roy and I fought like cat and dog. We'd been late leaving. In his usual laid-back style, Roy had left his packing to the last minute and then decided to cook himself fish for breakfast, which he'd proceeded to eat at a leisurely pace. He didn't believe we needed to get on the road early for the eight-hour drive and didn't think all my preparations were necessary. Just before we locked the house our chaffinch flew inside again. This time he went into the lounge and flew around my Buddhist altar.

This gave me pause, but soon Roy and I were bickering again. When I asked to make a toilet stop, he blamed me for distracting him so he missed a new speed limit sign. When we stopped there was an argument about whether I should withdraw cash at the supermarket or walk to an ATM. We moved on to fighting about buying Christmas presents for my family, and whether we should go to Tauranga after Cooks Beach to visit one of his friends.

It was a toxic blame game. Neither of us was right, yet we were convinced we were. Buddhists call this dwelling in a state of animalism. Yet waking up on our first morning at Cooks Beach, I felt a sense of relief. The bach where we were staying belonged to a friend's family. It was homely and comfortable, filled with the trappings of family holidays: piles of old *National Geographic* magazines, board games in cardboard boxes coming apart at the corners, kitchen cupboards filled with a mishmash of kitchenware. The beach, with its tame waves, was a block away.

I cooked pasta for dinner the night we arrived and vegetable curry the next. They were the first meals I'd cooked since JV died. These small acts reminded me I wasn't completely incapacitated. I realised why I'd wanted to leave Wellington so badly. I could leave my tormented self behind, shed it like a cocoon. I fantasised about staying at Cooks Beach forever, in the new clothes I was wearing.

During our second week at the beach there were two milestones: the Sunday marked five weeks since JV's birth, the Monday three weeks since his death. It was hard to know which was the more important. My darling boy. The way I thought about him had changed. In the first days after he died I could summon his face clearly in my mind's eye. Then, to my chagrin, I had to turn to photos. I still had moments when I palpably reconnected with him, as if I'd just been rocking him in my arms or stroking his forehead. In those moments I felt enormous tenderness, love, even peace. It was all the other moments – confusion, anxiety, disorientation – that were causing me problems. Where had this wicked mix of emotion come from? If only grief was a simple matter of sorrow and mourning.

During JV's life, before and after he was born, our lives were arranged around him. He had given me something to hope for, something to be strong for. What did I have to hope for and be strong for now?

I wondered if this was how a mountaineer felt after reaching a summit. You'd achieved your goal, and in the process spent all your available reserves of energy and adrenaline. When the cheering stopped, your injuries and pain became apparent. You were shattered, spent, broken. And you still had to climb back down the mountain. Hilary Mantel has written that we often have geographical associations with states of mind – buried memories, lofty thinking, spiralling downwards, feeling on a high. I wondered if I could find interviews with mountaineers to learn how they'd coped with difficult descents.

'It's like I want to renounce my whole life,' I told Viv, the counsellor at the hospice. I wanted Viv to explain myself to me. Were my riotous, chaotic feelings healthy or unhealthy? Normal or abnormal? Part of a recognised grieving process? Roy was responding in almost the opposite way. He was moving on, wanting to strengthen our life together, build on what we'd established. He spoke with great hope of our future as a couple.

Viv was reluctant to give an opinion. She came from the school of counselling that believed in listening without judging, allowing you to come to your own conclusions. Afterwards I went to the hospice chapel where there was a nativity scene made from knitted things, including baby Jesus in a basket. Of course, it was almost Christmas. We would see images of baby Jesus everywhere. It was nice to be in the chapel. I felt myself being lulled into a state of quietness.

'Hello, Emma.' I looked up and saw Chris, a spiritual adviser with whom I'd spoken a couple of times while we were in the hospice. 'You know, after you left one of the nurses commented that there was emptiness at the end of the hallway outside your room. It had been filled with love when you were here,' Chris said. "We were all so impressed by how you were with your baby, so caring and calm.'

I told Chris more about JV – receiving the diagnosis, the support we'd received from the Buddhist and Catholic communities. As I spoke I remembered how it felt to be with JV. 'I think we can honour him by healing,' I found myself saying. 'I want this experience to be the making of me, not the breaking. If part of my son's mission was to heal hearts, then surely that begins with mine and Roy's.'

Certainly this was something to aspire to, but it wasn't going to happen as fast as I wished. A few weeks later, we were driving to Auckland for Christmas. On the morning before we left Roy unexpectedly shaved his head. I went crazy when he emerged from the bathroom. I hated the way it looked. I hated that he hadn't told me he was going to do it. I hated that he'd chosen this moment to do it.

I knew he didn't deserve my violent reaction. I was afraid I'd destroy us if I continued this way. I was afraid of the places I was going to inside: unable to cope, joyless, uncomfortable in my skin, frightened. As we drove north, thoughts about how to free myself knifed at my insides. I wished I'd said no to buying the house.

* * *

Mum had built an altar by the Christmas tree, with candles and large photos of JV. She was honouring my son in a way I had been craving. She wore a beautiful necklace, a fine gold chain with a Hand of Fatima pendant, a symbol to ward off the evil eye that is often placed in babies' rooms.

On Christmas Eve I went alone to midnight mass. As the choir sang, 'The sweet baby Jesus lay down his sweet head' I pretended it was singing about my baby. In his sermon the priest said the most common words in the Bible were 'Don't be afraid.' Faith, he said, could make us less afraid. I knew I needed to feel less afraid. I needed to find a way to quell my incessant anxieties and anger, to be more like my son, like the chaffinch. To find peace in this strange and frightening time.

Later

In the weeks and months following JV's death I moved towards the peace I craved, but so slowly I sometimes didn't feel I was moving at all. Grief was bewildering and isolating. 'It's like being lost in fog in a foreign landscape and not being able to read the map to get out. Occasionally the fog parts and I see a little way forward. But I still don't know where I am or how long it will take me to navigate through this… let alone what state I'll be when I emerge,' I wrote in my journal in early January.

My mental disorientation was echoed by physical disorientation. For weeks, milk dripped from my breasts in the morning. My body was in a strange state – neither pregnant nor how it had been before pregnancy. None of my clothes hung right on my new baggy silhouette.

One of my strongest and most bewildering impulses continued to be to eschew everything around me. Later that month I wrote: 'I am trying not to be overwhelmed by all I wish to reject in my life. The house for one. The bloody house. And my paintings, clothes, office things, writing archives. My instinct is to rid myself of everything. As if it were possible to excommunicate myself from the context of my life. As if I could pluck from thin air a new wardrobe, new possessions, new everything.'

I had become judgemental of myself on all levels – homing in on my failures, seeing my successes as meagre. I was ambivalent about Roy's company, anyone's company. I couldn't be bothered replying to texts and emails. Socialising felt too great an effort. I found it hard to connect with my sense of love for JV, except for brief moments. I felt like I'd fallen from grace.

Looking for answers in cyberspace, I googled 'grief'. Websites such as *Psychology Today* gave bullet-pointed lists of the symptoms. They seemed too bald for what I was feeling. What was helpful was discovering pieces by writers. In a book review by Hilary Mantel on the *Guardian*'s website I stumbled across a quote from C.S. Lewis: 'No one ever told me that grief felt so like fear.' Lewis wondered whether a grieving person should be put in isolation, like a leper, to avoid the awkwardness of encounters with the unbereaved, who didn't know what to say and, although they felt goodwill, exhibited something like shame.

Mantel herself wrote: 'Grief is like fear in the way it gnaws the gut. Your mind is on a short tether, turning round and round. Your former life still seems to exist, but you can't get back to it; there is a glimpse in dreams of those peacock lawns and fountains, but you're fenced out.' Yes, that was just how I felt.

In her memoir about her mother's death Meghan O'Rourke wrote about a kind of numbness: 'I knew I was sad, but I knew it only intellectually. I couldn't feel it yet. It was like when you stay in cold water too long. You know something is off but don't start shivering for ten minutes.'

It was like that for me too. I rarely cried for JV, although I would have liked to. I was envious of Roy's grief and the way his tears flowed freely. Two hours later he would be ready to go to a neighbour's barbecue, while I would be sitting on the couch, jittery, numb, determined to go nowhere.

Would I always feel a hole inside that marked the absence of Jesús Valentino? A friend whose mother died suddenly when she was in her early twenties told me that ten years later the pain was still as raw and jagged as broken glass. 'But I wouldn't like her death not to hurt,' she explained. 'It hurts like this because I loved her so much.'

A book called *The Heart of Grief* by Thomas Attig offered a different perspective. Death, Attig wrote, wasn't an irrevocable separation because you could stay in a relationship with your loved one – through memories, through telling their story, through talking to their spirit if you believed that was possible.

'On Monday it was three months since our darling Jesús Valentino was born. His life was lived surrounded by people who loved and cared for him. He was only with us fifteen and a half days yet his entrance and exit from this world left something simple, pure and profound.'

I was speaking to a dozen of my work colleagues, who were standing in a huddle near the entrance to Zealandia. On a fence post next to me a small bronze plaque glinted in the sunlight. It was inscribed with our son's name and the dates of his birth and death. My colleagues had chipped in the money for this, a beautiful gesture.

I'd returned to my job in the middle of January, unsure if I was ready or able, but it had been the right decision. The routine of dressing, leaving the house, directing my thoughts to work, had been good. I transitioned from an acute stage of grief to feeling more like an empty husk. I wasn't exactly fun feeling like an empty husk but at least I wasn't the shattered mess I had been.

'I think your spirit tried to follow JV to the plane he was on. There is an energetic connection that exists between all mothers and babies after birth – stemming from the umbilical cord. In your case the umbilical cord is pulling tight and taut from your stomach, searching for JV.'

Barbara was a cranial sacral therapist. I lay on her table and she asked me to relax my lower back. This had been sore ever since the birth. As she did subtle manipulations I suddenly felt torrents of energy flow through me. I felt as if JV was with me again, as if I held him in my arms. I began to cry and felt in touch with a kind of sadness that had eluded me.

Afterwards I felt as though I were back inside my body again. It felt like a safe place, warm, comfortable, heavier, denser. With this came the sense I was willing to begin living my life again. On my way home I drove past the Home of Compassion. The garden was in darkness but a voice inside me said, 'Remember it still has the potential for glorious, fecund blooming.' I realised that although I had been moving through dark places, light would return. I smiled.

Since JV died nine babies had been born in our network of friends and acquaintances. Their parents had cautiously announced their pregnancies to me, worried the news would trigger feelings of loss or jealousy but they didn't. I never wished my baby was born healthy like theirs, I loved him for exactly who he was, which meant accepting his ectopia cordis heart.

As time went on, I was able to find sense in the chaos of grief. It was important for me to understand what had happened in the days when I felt so unstuck. I realised that the absolute love, the tenderness, the deep wish to care for my baby I had felt had all been cut short. My sense of being lost and despairing was linked to my thwarted desire to mother, protect and nurture. During pregnancy you experience the most intimate physical connection you can ever have with another human being, sharing your oxygen, blood, the space inside your skin. When a baby dies, it can feel a part of you has died with them. Yet it can be hard to channel your grief, to mourn a baby you have met only fleetingly. Who were they? What would they have become? You do not have years of life lived together to answer these questions.

I found it useful to read about how grief affects the brain. I learned that a part of the brain called the amygdala acts like a switching system, sending incoming information from our environment to the cortex. Here the information is processed, allowing us to decide whether a situation is safe or dangerous. With grief and trauma the amygdala can become overly sensitive and this can result in perception of threats where there are none, aggressive behavior, or withdrawing from others through fear. The amygdala also stimulates the production of cortisol, which in raised levels creates the 'fight or flight' response. When in fight or flight mode it is also common to feel disassociation – the brain shuts down emotions so you can deal with the threat at hand. For me the flight urge had been palpable: if I could have opened my wings and flown away from my life I would have.

A reaction to trauma, particularly where you have felt out of control, is to want to exert control over the things you can. JV's death had been out of my control. It had been followed swiftly by the purchase of a house, which I had felt unable to handle. There was a long list of things

I felt we needed to do to make the house a real home, yet while grieving I didn't have the energy, skills, or resources to do any of it, so I felt trapped and disempowered. Like the hard drive on a computer that shuts down when its memory banks are full, my unconscious was ordering me to eschew pressure and responsibilities.

A friend offered another theory: transference. Instead of being distressed about JV's death, I became distressed about our house. A house is a metaphor for self, a reflection of our identity, and I didn't want to be anchored in my world at all. In the end, though, the house represented acceptance of the present, the life we had. With slow sustained efforts, we began sorting, fixing and improving things. If I didn't love 6 Ariki Road, at least I could look on it dispassionately.

'JV, my boddhisatva, offered many lessons about living in the present with an open heart, trusting in the universe, giving and receiving love and compassion. My baby's life might have been brief, but he still had a soul mission.'

I was delivering a talk to a large gathering of Buddhists on a Sunday morning seven months after JV's death. Behind me, a photo of JV swaddled in his cream blanket and lying on his Peruvian poncho was projected on to a screen. It made him much bigger than in real life, bigger than me. I quoted the words of SGI's President Ikeda: 'confronting death at a fundamental level is an inevitable spiritual undertaking that helps us live more profoundly and meaningfully. We grasp the true meaning of life only when we honestly face the reality of death.' 'My baby's life and death represent one of the most profound experiences of my life to date,' I said.

When I finished, everyone stood and clapped. Someone I didn't know approached me and said he had seen JV standing beside me, no longer a baby but a fully fledged angel.

Do angels exist within the Buddhist universe? I would later ask a Buddhist leader this question. Her reply was that when we chant Nam-myoho-renge-kyo we are chanting to the universe in its entirety, so if angels exist we are chanting to them too. JV's life had bought me closer to Buddhism and closer to God and I liked the idea the two weren't mutually exclusive.

When I asked Father Lyons whether it was possible to practise Buddhism and believe in God, he said, 'Hmm, you always ask me the difficult questions. I would say yes, in that Buddhism and Catholicism are branches on the same tree, but it's important that you find your spiritual home.'

I could see his point. I'd wondered if believing in more than one religion or philosophy, hedging your bets, might dilute the strength of your faith. I'd found crossovers in the essential ideas of Buddhism and Catholicism, but also some fundamental differences. Buddhism emphasises that your state of consciousness can transform your life, while Catholicism places ultimate power in the hands of God. Yet I'd found myself open to both possibilities. Both traditions had helped me frame the events of JV's life and death in a way that helped me find meaning and made them more bearable. I'd experienced for the first time the way religious communities can mobilise support and compassion when you're facing tough times.

I spent some time trying to find a vessel in which to put a lock of JV's hair. I had in mind a glass vial I could wear on a necklace, but no amount of internet trawling unearthed one. In the end I settled on a tiny glass bottle, which I put inside a white leather pouch to wear around my neck whenever I wanted to hold JV's memory especially close.

A friend gave me a necklace with a silver heart engraved 'JV'. I wear it often. An uncle gave me a tiny diamond that had belonged to my paternal grandmother and I had it set in a ring. When I looked at it I was reminded of the Buddhist saying: 'Diamonds are forged under pressure.'

I sought other reminders, like ringing the wooden wind chimes Phoebe had given us, which we'd hung near photos of JV. When I rang them I would say my son's name.

In June we spoke at Sands' biennial conference in Wellington. Audience members were distinguishable by the colour of the lanyards worn around their necks – purple for bereaved families, orange for health professionals. Vicki Culling had asked Roy to be on a panel of fathers talking about grief and my mother and me to present a session on perinatal palliative care – the official term for care of a baby with a fatal condition. I began by saying, 'While perinatal palliative care was the right choice for my family, I respect the decision other families have made not to continue pregnancies on learning that all is not well with a baby. I believe in an ideal world our health system, families and communities would be flexible enough to support all choices around our precious babies' lives.'

I described our dealings with the hospital and the hospice. It felt empowering to be able to tell the health professionals in the audience what had helped and what hadn't. It was also special to be standing on the stage with my mother, and enlightening to hear things from her perspective. 'JV is my first grandchild,' she told the audience, 'and when Emma and Roy first told me they were expecting a baby, I was like any other expectant grandmother, my thoughts immediately thinking of a future with a little one in our family. Yes, the knitting started, and as I'm a keen cyclist I bought a little wooden bike for the new baby.

'As it started to become clear this baby was unlikely to survive the pregnancy, the knitting was put away, the bike was hidden, as I tried to find a way to support Emma and Roy through what I knew would be the hardest time in their lives.

'My learning, which I will take into my midwifery practice and into education of student midwives, is that parents in this situation need to know every option has been looked at, in order to be able to come to a balanced decision that's right for them. I think the option to continue a pregnancy needs to be reframed so that a time with a baby, however short, may for some families be precious and satisfying. People would say to me, "This must be so hard for you" but the fifteen and a half days I had with JV were the happiest of my life so far.'

When we finished speaking there were questions and comments. 'You've made a difference,' said a midwife, with tears in her eyes. 'You've been heard. This will change the way I do things.' I couldn't have hoped for better.

Afterwards it struck me how lucky we were to have lots of opportunities to share our son's story. I'd heard bereaved families speak about the loneliness of feeling as though their baby had been forgotten by the world. We were in almost the opposite situation. JV was known by many. Along with the talks I'd given, there had been articles about him in SGI's magazine and in the Catholic diocese newspaper. Dr W had also been in touch with a request.

I wanted to ask if you'd be happy to consider allowing me to publish a case report on JV, and the journey he had with us? I'd like to write something up for the Paediatric clinical literature as well as for the Palliative Care literature, if this is something you are happy with.

I think that it would be extremely helpful for clinicians caring for similar babies in the future to have the opportunity to read about how we cared for JV, and what can be done with a multi-disciplinary team. As you know, there's very little useful published information out there. … But really – if you're not comfortable – that's absolutely OK too.

In addition Tisha had asked our permission to do a presentation on JV and our family at a neonatal nurses' conference. We agreed to both those things – sharing JV's story felt like a way to honour his life and for further value to come of it. My only concern was that I didn't want photos shown of JV with his heart exposed. I feared they might find their way on to the internet like a freak show.

Getting JV's headstone made took months. In the meantime I covered his small plot with a cream laminated sheet printed with an ornate gold pattern and pinned down with tent pegs. Next to a small temporary plaque printed with his name I stuck bunches of plastic flowers into the ground – pink, white and yellow. I'd seen graves decorated like this in Tonga, gorgeously festooned with colourful woven mats and flowers. The cemeteries there made you smile.

The headstone was silver-grey granite. Encircling the grave was a low border and inside it we planted a white rose bush chosen by my mother. The border itself was decorated with hand-painted ceramic tiles. Katherine Smythe, a local ceramicist, had offered to source the tiles for free and let me to use her studio, where she would provide special glazes and fire the tiles. For a month I went to her studio once a week. I painted thirty tiles in glazes of pale blue, rose red and lilac, with hearts, crosses, lotus flowers and doves, and Spanish words: Esperanza (Hope), Corazon (Heart). Some tiles had a mixture of symbols, like a coat of arms, reflecting JV's Buddhist and Catholic heritage.

The stonemason who made the headstone and border hadn't ever tiled a grave so he suggested we employ a professional tiler or do it ourselves.

We decided on the do-it-yourself method. On the scheduled day it was windy and grey clouds threatened. This was a problem: the grout needed to remain dry for a period of time to set well. As Roy quickly slapped down the tiles, I clambered behind him with a rag wiping up the excess grout. In the end the rain held off and tiles were clean and perfectly placed. We agreed the grave looked wonderful.

'Emsy, you did such a good job you should be an architect,' Roy said, and gave me a kiss on the cheek.

'Thanks, Roycito,' I said.

We were in a good place in our relationship. I was grateful we'd managed to get through the tough phase after JV died. I'd read that after the death of a baby couples are more likely to separate and I could understand why. In the midst of grief I'd hardly been a loving companion. Now, though, the events of the last eighteen months had solidified our partnership. I'd begun to feel excited about our future.

JV's grave unveiling was held on November 8, 2015, close to the first anniversary of his death. On a blustery Sunday fifty of our family and friends gathered at the cemetery. Father Lyons said a prayer. Roy and I spoke. Phoebe and my brother Alex, who was visiting from Ireland, sang JV's songs – '¿Cómo estás, Jesús Valentino?' and 'This Little Light Of Mine'.

I knew by then I was nearly twelve weeks pregnant. I thought about announcing this but decided against it: I didn't want the news to become the focus. This baby wouldn't be a replacement for JV, or a silver lining that made everything better. He or she would be loved as their own person with their own distinct story. All going well, of course. I had not yet had the twelve-week scan and knew better than to take anything for granted.

On the actual anniversary of JV's death we spontaneously decided to visit the Mary Potter Hospice. By a stroke of good luck, our room was empty. One year later we were in the space where JV had lived and died. I sat in the chair by the window where I'd rocked him and given him bottles. Roy stood holding the metal frame of the bed where we'd lain next to him.

By chance, that day, at the very hour of JV's death, Tisha was doing her presentation at the nurses' conference. 'By the end everyone was crying, including me,' she told us afterwards. 'They wanted to pass on their thanks to you for sharing the story.' She won a prize for the best presentation. I was proud of my darling son and the ripples his life still created.

Two years later

'Blow out the candles, darling!'

I'd baked a cake to celebrate JV's birthday. Our son Amaru Gabriel, born healthy and well in 2016, was sixteen months old and dazzled by the idea of cake for breakfast. That day we visited Yayoi Kusama's exhibition 'Life is the heart of a rainbow', where an entire room was covered in multicoloured dots. Viewers were invited to add to the explosion of colour by placing more dot stickers. I found a small area of white wall and spelled out 'JV'.

We were now living in Brisbane, where Roy had a job at a university research institute. We were enjoying being woken up in the morning by cackling kookaburras, eating endless mangoes, walking in bright sunshine, making discoveries. We had begun a new chapter in our life but JV remained a central character. When people asked me how many children I had, I always said two. I didn't like to say I'd lost a baby, because JV didn't feel lost to me. Sometimes he felt very close. My memories of him were like reflections of light on water, or fragments of colour turning in a kaleidoscope. I got glimpses, the pattern held for a moment. Sometimes something touched the place in me where Jesús Valentino resided, a touch as gentle as a rose petal brushing a cheek, and I would feel the wonder of holding him in my arms again.